THE GAMES WE PLAYED

THE

WE

PLAYED

THE
GOLDEN AGE
OF BOARD & TABLE GAMES

MARGARET K. HOFER

with a foreword by

KENNETH T. JACKSON

from the
NEW-YORK HISTORICAL SOCIETY'S LIMAN COLLECTION

PRINCETON ARCHITECTURAL PRESS
NEW YORK

PUBLISHED BY
PRINCETON ARCHITECTURAL PRESS
37 EAST SEVENTH STREET
NEW YORK, NEW YORK 10003

For a free catalog of books, call 1.800.722.6657.
Visit our Web site at www.papress.com.

This book was inspired by The Games We Played: American Board and Table
Games from the Liman Collection Gift, *an exhibition held at the New-York*
Historical Society from April 2, 2002 to April 13, 2003.

Editing: Nancy Eklund Later
Design: John Clifford
Cover Design: Deb Wood
Photography: Glenn Castellano

Special thanks to: Nettie Aljian, Ann Alter, Nicola Bednarek, Janet Behning,
Megan Carey, Penny Chu, Russell Fernandez, Jan Haux, Clare Jacobson, Mark Lamster,
Linda Lee, Nancy Levinson, Katharine Myers, Jane Sheinman, Scott Tennent,
and Jennifer Thompson of Princeton Architectural Press
—Kevin C. Lippert, publisher

Library of Congress Cataloging-in-Publication Data

Hofer, Margaret K., 1965–
The games we played : the golden age of board and table games /
Margaret K. Hofer ; with a foreword by Kenneth T. Jackson.—1st ed.
p. cm.
"Inspired by ... an exhibition held at the New-York Historical Society
from April 2, 2002, to January 5, 2003"—T.p. verso.
Includes bibliographical references (p.).
ISBN 1-56898-397-2 (alk. paper)
1. Board games—History. I. Title.
GV1317 .H64 2003
794—dc21

2002154489

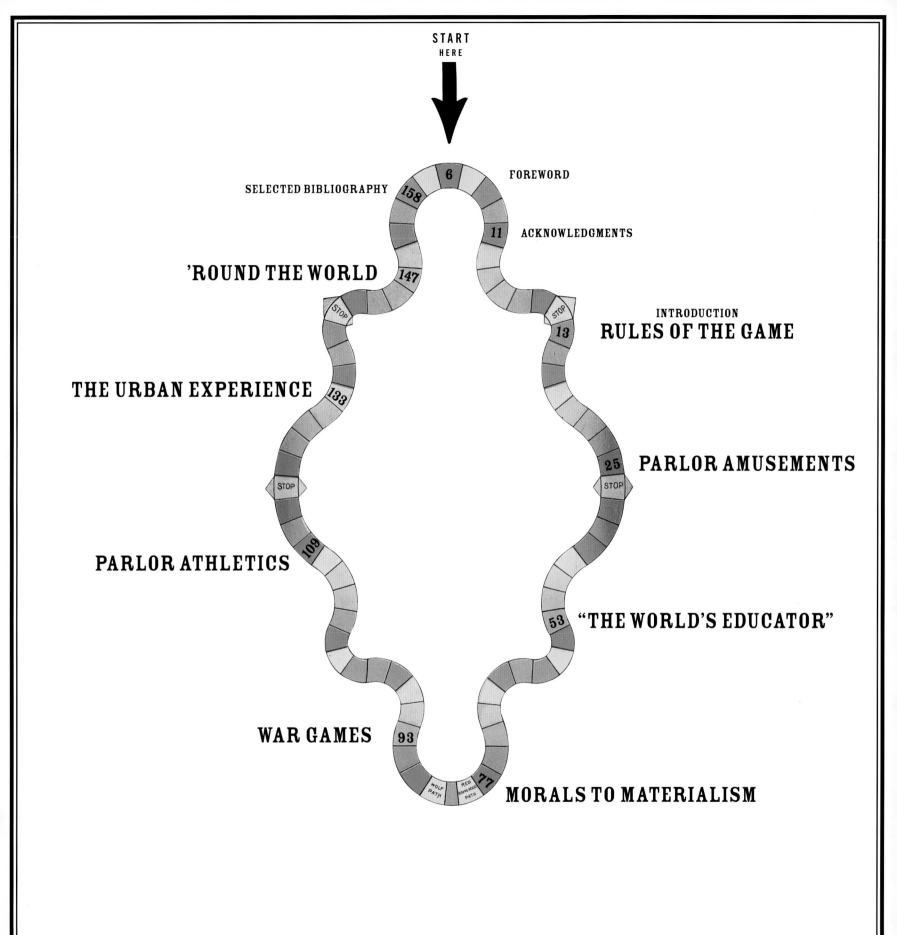

START
HERE

STOP

STOP

STOP

STOP

WOLF
PATH

RED
RIDING HOOD
PATH

For almost six decades, I have been playing and enjoying board games, especially those like *Monopoly*, *Scrabble*, or *Trivial Pursuit* that allow some combination of luck, strategy, and knowledge to give their players the kinds of clear victories and successes that are so rare in real life. When I win, which is not frequent, I allow myself the delusion that, but for chance, I could have been a billionaire real estate developer or a televised winner on *Jeopardy*. And even when the cards or the chips or the dice betray me, I can at least enjoy inexpensive excitement and competition, where the playing surface is flat, where conditions are equal for everyone, and where it matters not whether you are skinny or fat, young or old, male or female, or physically handicapped.

In all my years of ferocious game playing, however, it never occurred to me that the board games themselves could be considered historical artifacts and that they might be examined analytically, especially in terms of how they reflect the times in which they were created. Fortunately, Ellen and Arthur Liman had more imagination than I did. On a whim, they purchased a timeworn British map puzzle for six dollars at a yard sale in 1980. An accomplished artist, Ellen began a long journey of searching out and purchasing historic board and table games, drawn to their extraordinary designs, vivid colors, and overall aesthetic impression. Ultimately, the couple's extensive collection included rare, hand-tinted games as well as magnificently illustrated examples, the depth of detail and sophisticated colors of which were made possible by chromolithographic printing.

For Arthur Liman, who was by 1980 one of the nation's most respected and successful attorneys, the appeal of the games lay in their reflection of American history and popular culture. Donated to the New-York Historical Society in 2000, the Liman Collection constitutes a rich resource for exploring our changing values, aspirations, and prejudices, and for revealing the myriad ways that political events, technological achievements, and ordinary domestic life were revealed in the games people played. Whatever its theme, each game in some way reflects the customs and concerns of middle- and upper-class Americans, who were dealing with immigration, industrialization, urbanization, and globalization a century and more ago.

Arthur and Ellen Liman spent two decades scouring flea markets, attic sales, and auctions to assemble their acclaimed collection of board games. This unusual volume presents well over one hundred of these remarkable objects, drawn from the more than five hundred American board and table games given to the New-York Historical Society by the Limans. Here, as in the Society, they are presented to future generations of (vicarious) players to ponder and enjoy.

Cordially,
Kenneth T. Jackson

Game of the
MAN *in the* **MOON**

McLoughlin Brothers
New York, N.Y., copyright 1901

LOST *in the* WOODS
McLoughlin Brothers
New York, N.Y., circa 1890

ACKNOWLEDGMENTS

Manufactured during the late-nineteenth century—the golden age of board and table games—the remarkable artifacts in this comprehensive collection were gathered by astute collectors Ellen Liman and her late husband Arthur. Their deep knowledge of the subject, trained eyes, and persistent pursuit of games provided the foundation for this volume and for the exhibition that inspired it, which was held at the New-York Historical Society in 2002 and 2003 to celebrate the Limans' monumental gift.

The Games We Played is the product of a collaborative undertaking. Key players include Jennifer Jensen, whose painstaking cataloging of the Liman Collection provided the groundwork for developing the exhibition and book, and co-curator Amy Weinstein, whose experienced eye and exacting research made her an ideal partner in shaping the exhibition. I am indebted to my colleagues at the New-York Historical Society, whose teamwork and strategy helped to produce a winning exhibition. I am also grateful to Glenn Castellano for his stunning photographs of the games and to Nancy Eklund Later, editor at Princeton Architectural Press, for recognizing the publishing potential of the Liman Collection, conceiving this book, and providing unflagging enthusiasm from start to finish. Finally, I owe my deepest gratitude to my husband Andrew, who throughout the project kept me on track with humor, patience, and loving support.

Margaret K. Hofer

RULES
OF THE
GAME

The games that entertained Americans from the 1840s to the 1920s offer a fascinating window on the values, beliefs, and aspirations of a nation undergoing tremendous change. During this period the United States experienced a shift from predominantly agrarian to urban living, strained to absorb millions of new immigrants, and ascended to international commercial power. As the nation grew increasingly urban and industrialized, the spheres of home and workplace became more distinct. The American home, no longer the heart of economic production, became the center of education, entertainment, and moral enlightenment. Middle-class families—with expanded leisure time as well as rising income levels—embraced leisure pursuits in the home and encouraged their children to play games that would develop skills and provide moral instruction.

During the same period in history, several significant cultural and technological developments combined to produce a revolution in the manufacture of American board games. Improvements in printing and paper making enabled the large-scale commercial production of board games. Most important were advances in chromolithography, a color printing process perfected in the 1870s that created bold, richly colored images at affordable prices. A typical middle-class household of the time could readily purchase such games, the prices of which ranged from 25 cents for small boxed card games to three dollars or more for elaborate editions.

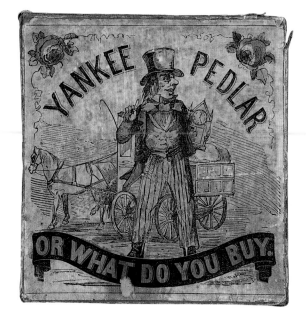

LEFT: The charming hand-colored engravings of *Yankee Pedlar, or What Do You Buy?* (John McLoughlin), were executed in New York around 1850.

PAGE 12: *The Game of John Gilpin* was manufactured by McLoughlin Brothers about 1880, the heyday of American board and table game production.

The game boards and boxes collected here graphically illustrate the changes effected by the chromolithography revolution. Early games, such as *Yankee Pedlar, or What Do you Buy?* (circa 1850), tended to be small and were produced by hand-coloring a monochrome print. This time-consuming and expensive process was typically executed by factory workers, usually low-paid young girls. As manufacturers adapted chromolithography to board game production in the 1870s, board game boxes grew larger and more colorful, often featuring bold graphics. By the mid-1880s, New York City-based McLoughlin Brothers (active 1858–1920) dominated the industry with sumptuous, eye-catching packaging that was frequently more compelling than the games it contained.

The box cover of *The Game of Playing Department Store* (McLoughlin Brothers, copyright 1898) demonstrates the bold, vivid chromolithography characteristic of the best nineteenth-century board games.

New York City, the nation's business capital, emerged as the leading center of American chromolithography and the hub of the nation's vigorous board game industry. The earliest game known to have been produced in America, *Traveller's Tour through the United States*, was made by a New York City bookseller in 1822. During the height of board game popularity in the late-nineteenth century, the nation's leading manufacturers, such as McLoughlin Brothers, maintained prominent retail stores on lower Broadway, the city's main shopping thoroughfare. In addition to McLoughlin Brothers, whose name became synonymous with family entertainment, important New York City toy and game manufacturers included Selchow & Righter, J. H. Singer, E. I. Horsman, J. Ottmann, and Clark & Sowdon, as well as S. L. Hill of Brooklyn. Large game companies located outside New York, like Massachusetts-based Milton Bradley and Parker Brothers, maintained branch offices in Manhattan to take advantage of the brisk urban marketplace. The golden age of board and table games flourished until shortly after the turn of the twentieth century, when the creative and artistic zeal fueling the industry

After Milton Bradley acquired McLoughlin Brothers in 1920, the firm reproduced a few McLoughlin games under its own label. *The Game of Mail, Express or Accommodation*, originally copyrighted by McLoughlin Brothers in 1895, was updated with a new box cover featuring a bold, streamlined design more likely to appeal to modern consumers.

gradually dwindled. The era officially drew to a close with Milton Bradley's acquisition of McLoughlin Brothers in 1920.

Games did not always find easy acceptance. In seventeenth- and eighteenth-century America, agrarian life left little time for leisure pursuits, and games were viewed with some suspicion. Puritans frowned on gaming and considered dice instruments of the devil. Some Americans, however, did enjoy amusements, such as card playing, horse racing, skittles and other bowling games, and gambling.

Many of the games that captured the interest of Americans had been played by various cultures for centuries: *Draughts*, or *Checkers*, was played in ancient Greece and Rome; *Fox and Geese* puzzled the English as far

Children schooled in Greek mythology would have recognized references in McLoughlin Brothers' *Game of the Spider's Web* (copyright 1898) to the story of Arachne, a beautiful maiden frightened by the jealous goddess Athena, who turned her into a spider.

as the fifteenth century; the ancient game of *Parcheesi* entertained royalty in sixteenth-century India; and *Lotto* was played in Genoa in the seventeenth century. Through the mid-nineteenth century, most games were imported from England, and the first games of American manufacture, such as *The Mansion of Happiness* (1843), were exact copies or direct derivations of English games. By the 1880s, game manufacturers had forged products with a distinct American identity, using subject matter that embodied the character of the nation.

The majority of games produced during the golden age of game manufacturing—from the 1880s until just after the turn of the century—are games of chance requiring little or no skill of their players.

By far the most common type is the race or track game, in which competitors vie to be the first to reach a designated goal. Players advance randomly by a flick of the spinner or spin of the teetotum (a top-like device with numbers); later, as Americans relaxed their views on gaming, dice also became key game accessories. Games demanding strategic skill were produced in fewer numbers, although some games used a combination of skill and chance. Dexterity games challenging players' manual skill, such as *Fish Pond* and *Tiddledy Winks*, and quiz games testing factual knowledge enjoyed great popularity during this period.

As the twentieth century unfolded, the arrival of radio and television in American homes dampened the success of the games industry, but board

LEFT: As dice were associated with gambling, many nineteenth-century game players opted for amusements that employed a teetotum to determine their moves.

RIGHT: Introduced in the 1870s and popular for more than a decade, folding "bookshelf" games combine three games in one. When folded closed and placed on a shelf, they resemble the spine of a book—a telling feature that betrays a lingering ambivalence about gaming. On the reverse of the *Game of John Gilpin* (McLoughlin Brothers, circa 1880) are *Rainbow Backgammon* and *Bewildered Travelers*.

games remained a staple of wholesome family fun and "edu-tainment." Many of today's favorites trace their roots to games first introduced in the nineteenth century: the chestnut *Monopoly*, debuted in 1935, is derived from games of the 1880s based on the accumulation of wealth, such as *Monopolist* and *Bulls and Bears: The Great Wall St. Game*. *The Game of Life* is an updated version of *The Checkered Game of Life* issued in 1960 to celebrate the classic game's centennial, and the popular *Trivial Pursuit* is a direct descendant of parlor quiz games such as *The World's Educator*. The perennial favorite *Scrabble*, found in one of every three American homes today, is based on *Anagrams*, a game popular at the turn of the century. Other games produced during

The object of *Jim Crow Ten Pins* (J. Ottmann Lith. Co., circa 1900), a target game, was to knock down smiling minstrel figures with a bowling ball.

the late-nineteenth century are unfamiliar or even abhorrent to current sensibilities. The phrases prescribed in conversation games, intended for a generation of Americans accustomed to highly structured social interaction, seem trite and insipid today. The bluntness and cruelty of racist games, on the other hand, are shocking to modern viewers.

In times of crisis, Americans have found relief in the distraction and companionship of board game pursuits. At the outbreak of the Civil War, sales of board games soared as families turned inward to grapple with the deep split wrenching the nation. During the war's first winter season, *The Checkered Game of Life* sold an unprecedented 40,000 copies. Most recently, in the wake of September 11, 2001, traditional games experienced another surge in popularity, as family and friends came together to cope with the tragedy and find consolation and strength within their intimate kinship circles.

The following thematic chapters explore games as a unique cultural mirror reflecting American values and beliefs. As the informal face of culture, games offer less self-conscious, and hence more accurate, revelations about the society they entertained. The examples illustrated here expose the nation's competitive spirit and the distinctly American ideal of success, communicate the country's pride in its expanding borders and technological achievements, reveal beliefs about the educational and moral development of children, and even betray a fascination with spiritualism and the occult. They reveal the hopes and fears of Americans at the turn of the twentieth century, just as today's popular games— *Monopoly*, *Cranium*, and even *Pokémon*—will reveal those of Americans at the dawn of the twenty-first century to future generations.

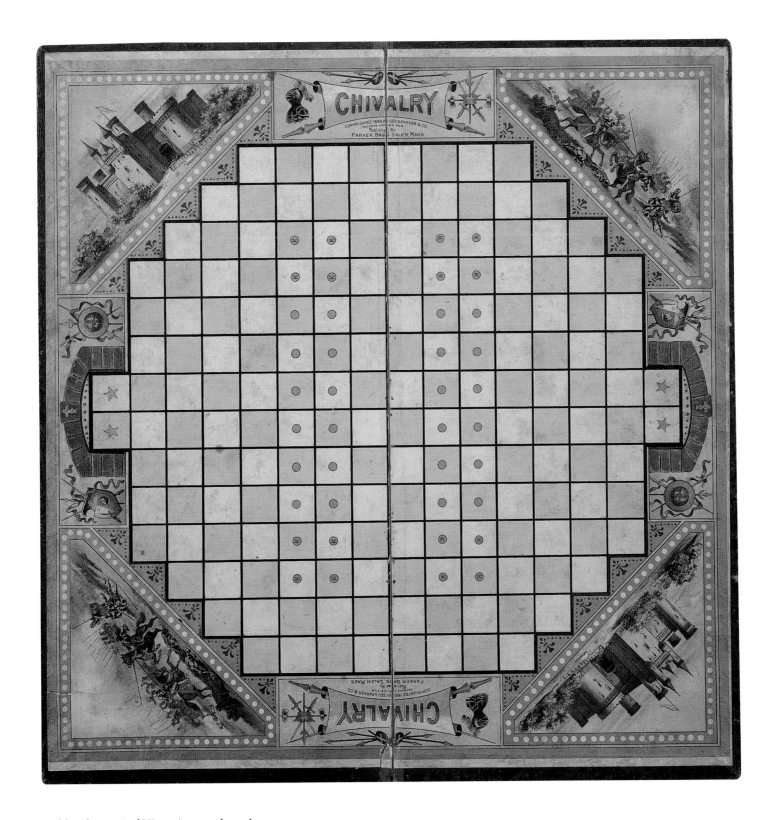

Unlike the typical Victorian-era board games,
Chivalry (Parker Brothers, copyright 1888)
had complex rules and demanded strategic
skill to win.

1

PARLOR
AMUSEMENTS

For middle- and upper-class Americans in the second half of the nineteenth century, the parlor was the anchor of family life. Before the advent of radio, television, and video games, families spent much of their leisure time assembled in the parlor, conversing, reading, writing, and playing games of all kinds. Whether elegant or humble, the focal point of any proper parlor was its center table. Placed in the middle of the room, the circular table provided a practical function, allowing the shared use of a single lighting source in an era when artificial lighting was expensive. Over time, the center table itself came to symbolize the family circle.

Many parlor games conceived in the nineteenth century continue to entertain American families today, although they are more likely enjoyed around the kitchen table or spread out on the living room floor. Card games such as *Old Maid*, letter games such as *Anagrams*, and dexterity games such as *Jack Straws* (today's *Pick Up Sticks*) are enduring favorites. Other parlor games that have since fallen out of favor provide telling insights into Victorian culture. The popularity of fortune-telling games involving mysticism, for instance, attests to nineteenth-century Americans' fascination with magic and the occult, while the endless variety of conversation games reveals a reliance on structured and controlled social interaction.

PAGE 24
Game of **LOTTO**
McLoughlin Brothers
New York, N.Y., copyright 1897

LEFT
The **PRETTY VILLAGE**
McLoughlin Brothers
New York, N.Y., copyright 1890
Children could create imaginary towns with the easy-to-assemble buildings in *The New Pretty Village*. The quaint structures in this popular game reflect a new nostalgia for a simple, agrarian past.

RIGHT
The New **PRETTY VILLAGE**
McLoughlin Brothers
New York, N.Y., copyright 1897

THE NEW PRETTY VILLAGE

MOTHER GOOSE'S PARTY,
or The Merry Game of OLD MAID
McLoughlin Brothers
New York, N.Y., copyright 1887

Pussy-cat, pussy-cat, where have you been?
I've been to London to visit the Queen!
Pussy-cat, pussy-cat, what did you there?
I frighten'd a little mouse under her chair.

Peter, Peter, pumpkin eater,
Had a wife and couldn't keep her—
He put her in a pumpkin shell,
And there he kept her very well.

Goosey, goosey, gander, whither shall I wander?

Up-stairs, and down-stairs, and in my lady's chamber

Little Jack Horner sat in a corner,
    Eating a Christmas pie;
He put in his thumb, and he took out a plum,
    And said: "What a good boy am I!"

There was a piper had a cow,
    And he had naught to give her;
He pull'd out his pipes and play'd her a tune,
    And bade the cow consider.

This little pig goes to market.

BE A DUDE

BE SLOVENLY

BE ILL-TEMPERED

BE A CRANK

The Game of **DONT'S**
and **OLD MAID**

McLoughlin Brothers
New York, N.Y., copyright 1905

Old Maid, a turn-of-the-century favorite, was based on the notion that remaining unmarried was a woman's worst fate.

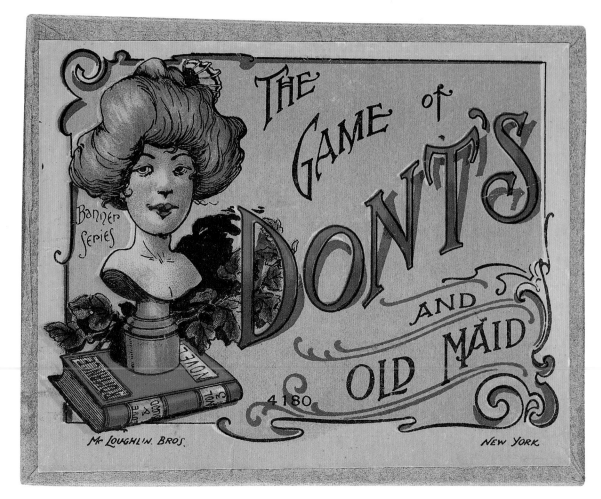

McLoughlin Brothers
New York, N.Y., copyright 1890

JOEL GRABB,
Dr. Fusby's Landlord.

DR. FUSBY.

MARTHA FUSBY,
The Doctor's Wife.

DICK FUSBY,
The Doctor's Son.

JACOB SLY,
Dr. Fusby's Lawyer.

JANE OX,
The Butcher's Wife.

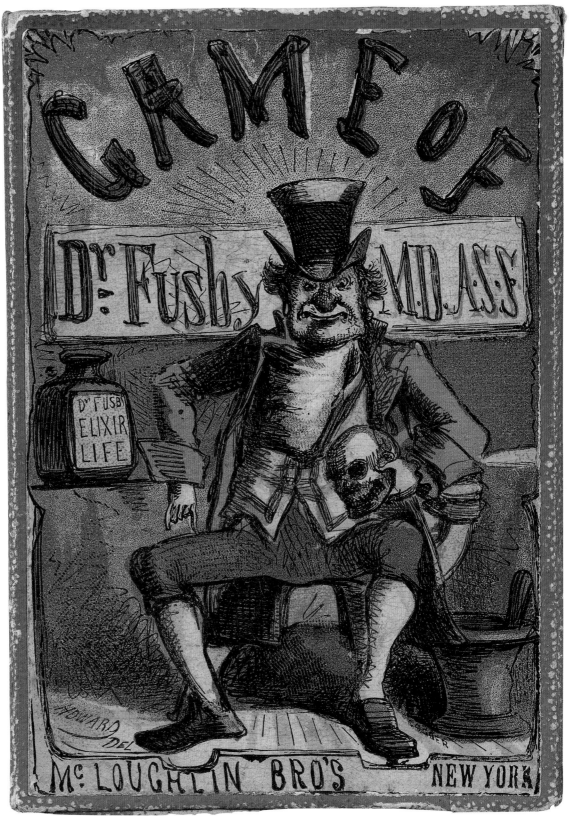

The Improved Game of
SNAP

McLoughlin Brothers
New York, N.Y., copyright 1889

In the enduring card game *Snap*, players turn
over cards from their hand and call out "snap!"
when they see a matched pair.

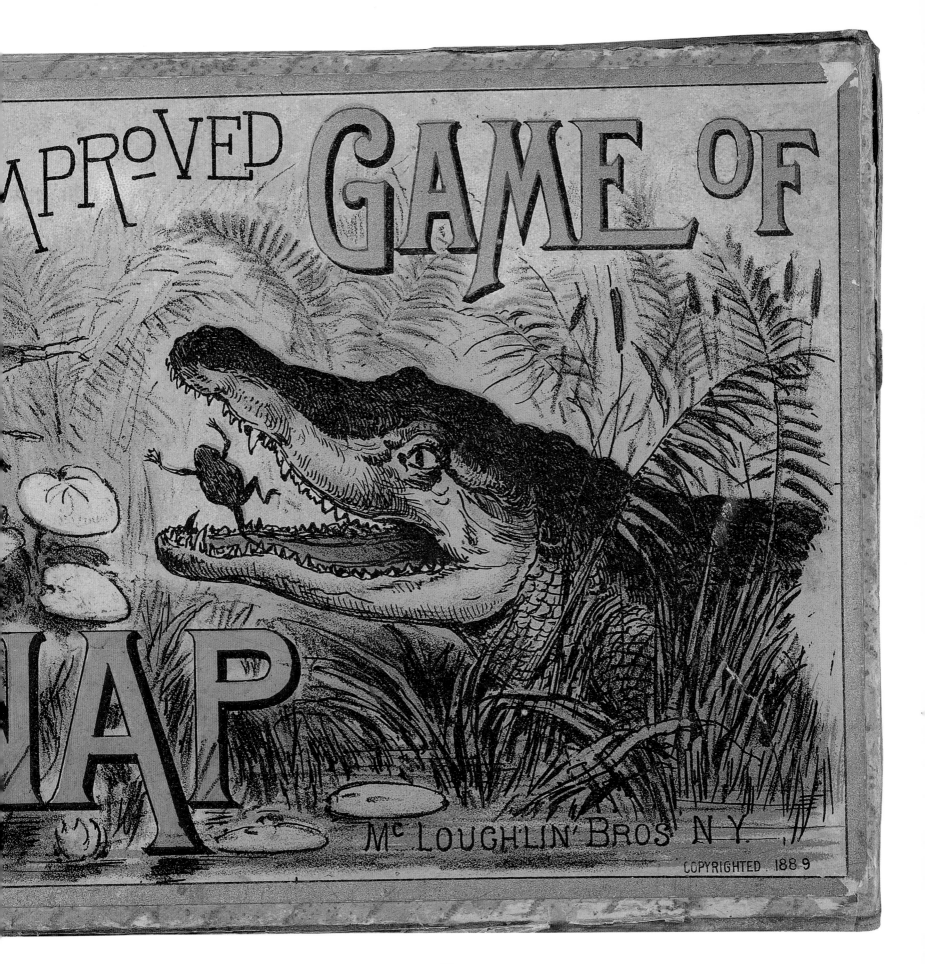

IMPROVED GAME OF

GAME OF

SNAP

MᶜLoughlin Bros. N.Y.

COPYRIGHTED 1889

The Premium Game
LOGOMACHY,
or WAR *of* WORDS
McLoughlin Brothers
New York, N.Y., 1889

ANAGRAMS
and Other Letter Games

Milton Bradley Co.
Springfield, Mass., circa 1910

Anagrams was one of several word-building games that gained popularity around the turn of the twentieth century. Players create words from tiles selected at random from the box and attempt to "capture" the most words to win the game.

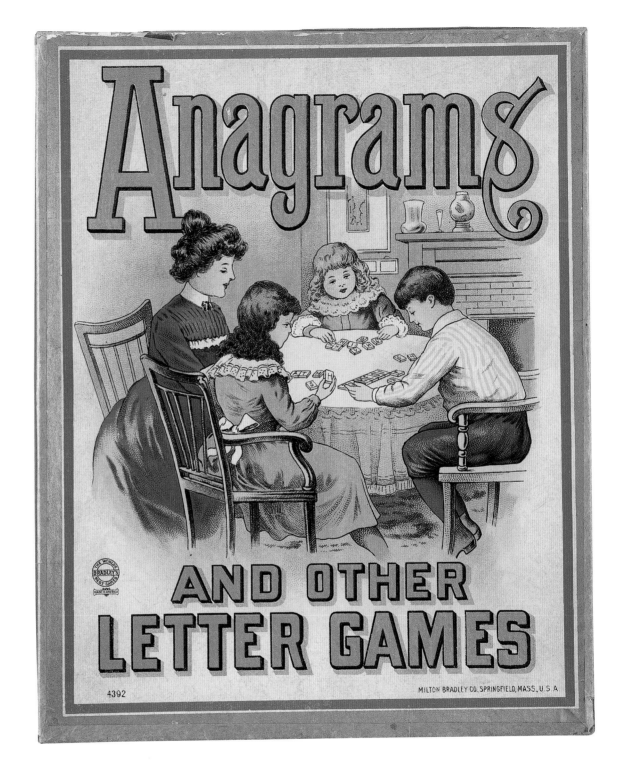

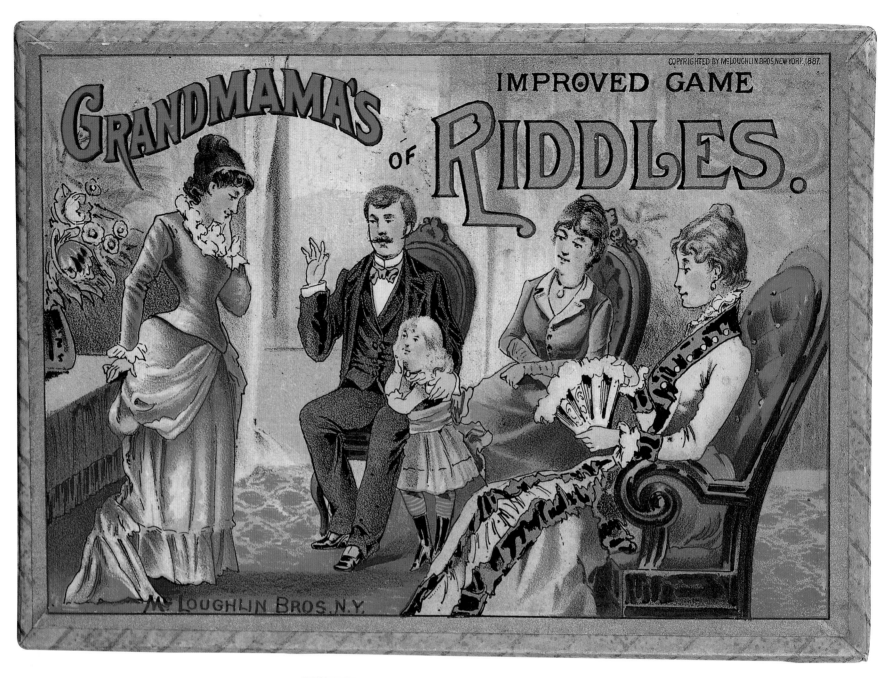

Grandmama's Improved Game of
RIDDLES

McLoughlin Brothers
New York, N.Y., copyright 1887

Players of *Grandmama's Riddles* compete to answer the most number of riddles correctly. Solutions to the riddles are read by one player, dubbed the "Preceptor," from the accompanying book of answers.

> 50.
> What word is that to which, if you add a syllable, will make it shorter?

Short (shorter.)

> 61.
> When is a dog's tail not a dog's tail?

When it is a—wagon (wagging.)

> 16.
> Why is your nose like St. Paul's?

Because it is flesh and blood.

MIXED PICKLES

SELCHOW & RIGHTER
NEW YORK, N.Y., CIRCA 1890

Players of *Mixed Pickles* create an original story by combining phrases contained on game cards. The accompanying instructions assure players that they will be "convulsed with laughter at the ludicrous combination of sentences."

I'm always in for

Hunting buffaloe

At a wedding

Komikal
KONVERSATION KARDS
SELCHOW & RIGHTER
NEW YORK, N.Y., CIRCA 1893

As a way of differentiating their product from McLoughlin's *Comical Conversation Cards,* and also as an attention-grabbing ploy, Selchow & Righter opted for a humorous misspelling of the game's title.

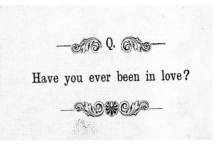

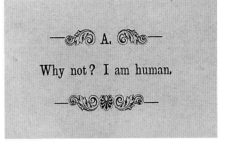

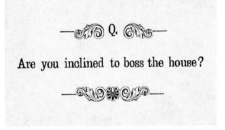

The Elite
CONVERSATION CARDS
McLoughlin Brothers
New York, N.Y., copyright 1887

Courting couples uncomfortable with romantic conversation could break the ice with conversation cards, which contained humorous or flirtatious questions and answers. McLoughlin Brothers promoted the cards by claiming that "to bashful people they are a great blessing, not only furnishing an hour's amusement, but sometimes leading them to the gates of matrimony."

ABOVE
THE SOCIABLE TELEPHONE

ABOVE

THE SOCIABLE TELEPHONE

J. Ottmann Lith. Co.

New York, N.Y., copyright 1902

Toward the end of the nineteenth century, Americans were preoccupied with questions of proper social behavior and enjoyed numerous games providing structured social interaction. In *Sociable Telephone*, players connected by a "telephone" (two wooden blocks connected by a string) pose questions that must be answered with the humorous sentences on the game cards.

RIGHT

WHAT'S HIS NAME?

Parker Brothers

Salem, Mass., copyright 1902

S

1. An English Poet.
   Born April, 1564; died
   April 23, 1616.
   WILLIAM SHAKESPEARE.

2. Famous English Explorer.
   Born 1841.
   HENRY M. STANLEY.

3. A Scotch Novelist.
   Born Aug. 15, 1771; died
   Sept. 21, 1832.
   SIR WALTER SCOTT.

A

1. An American President.
   Born Oct. 30, 1735; died
   July 4, 1826.
   JOHN ADAMS.

2. An American Patriot.
   Born Jan. 10, 1737; died
   Feb. 13, 1789.
   ETHAN ALLEN.

3. A great American Naturalist.
   Born May 4, 1780; died
   Jan. 27, 1851.
   JOHN J. AUDUBON.

R

1. An American President.
   Born Oct. 27, 1858.
   THEODORE ROOSEVELT.

2. A famous Dutch Artist.
   Born July 15, 1607; died
   Oct. 8, 1669.
   HERMANZOON VAN RYN
   REMBRANDT.

3. A Diamond King (English).
   Born 1853; died March,
   1902.
   CECIL J. RHODES.

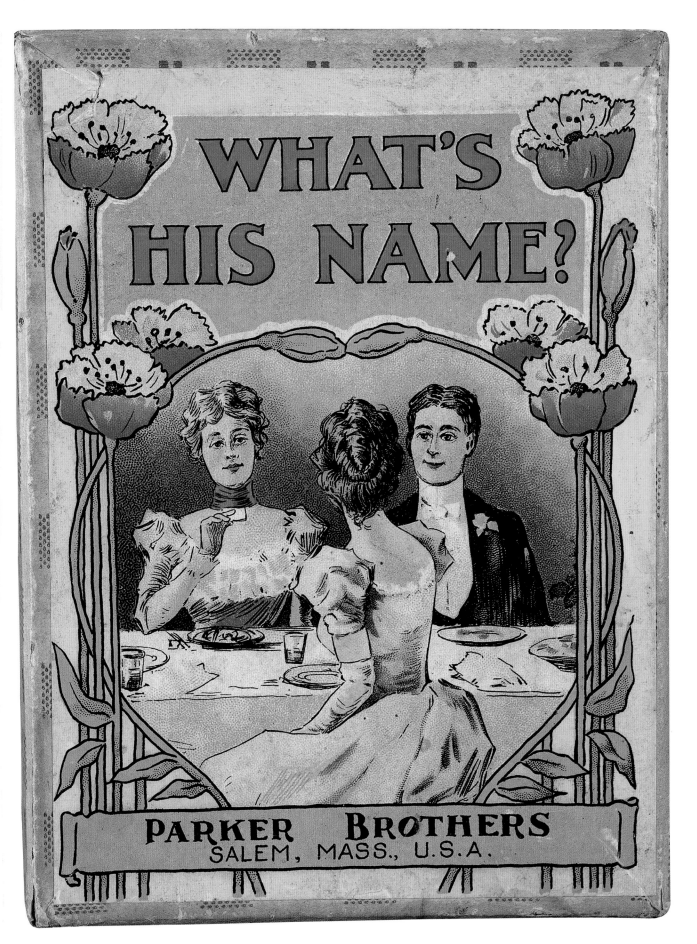

WHAT'S HIS NAME?

PARKER BROTHERS
SALEM, MASS., U.S.A.

55 21 24 53 28

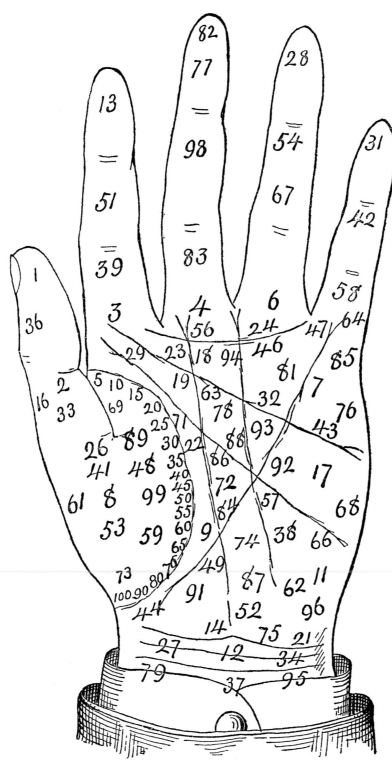

PALMISTRY

MANUFACTURER UNKNOWN
UNITED STATES, CIRCA 1910

While loosely based on the principles of palmistry, this game is aimed more at amusing players than instructing them in palm reading. Players draw numbered cards and read their corresponding indication in the accompanying booklet. Lucky players learn of their longevity and good fortune; others might be exposed as gluttons, opium addicts, or "excessive onion eaters." The player receiving the greatest number of complimentary indications wins the game.

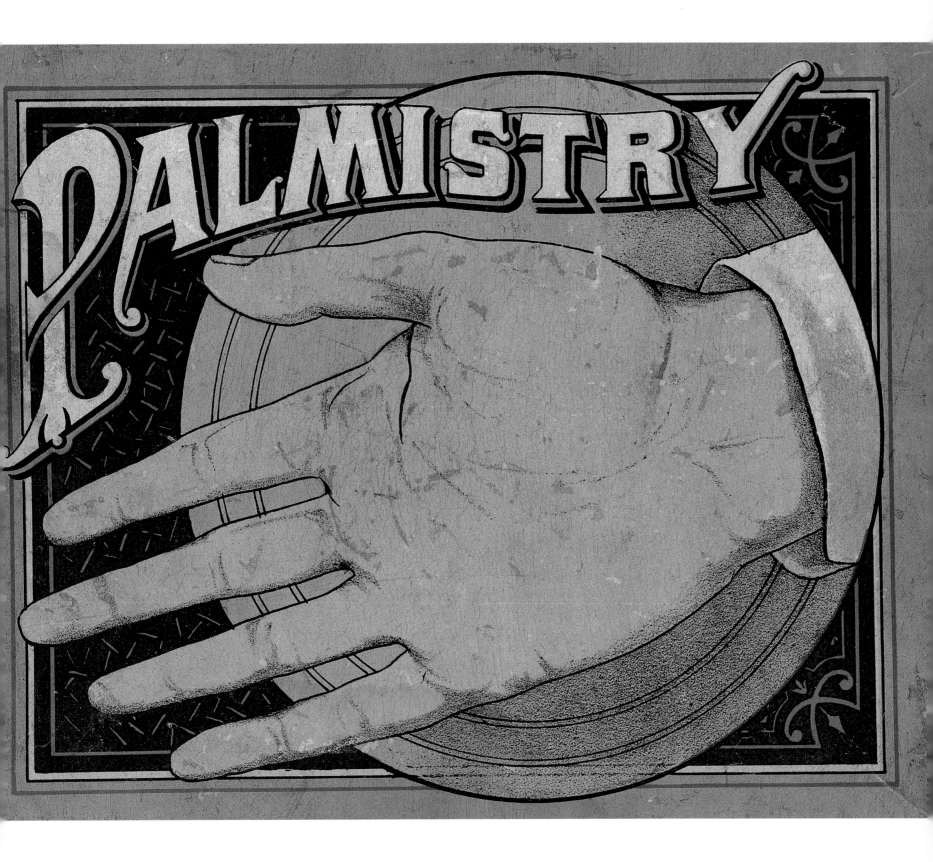

Eyes.

Whiskers.

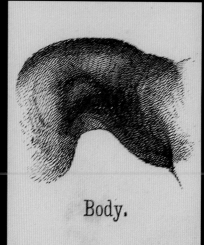

Body.

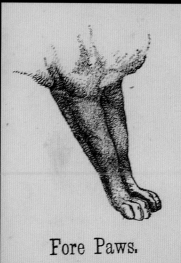

Fore Paws.

THE BLACK CAT

Fortune Telling Game

PARKER BROTHERS

SALEM, MASS., 1897

12.
Your Destiny.
ZINNIA.

LADY.

Be thou chaste as ice, as pure as snow,
Thou shalt not escape calumny.
SHAKSPEARE.

GENT.

To cast and balance at a desk,
Perched like a crow upon a three-legged
stool.
TENNYSON.

6.
Your Character.
CHINA ASTER.

LADY,

The world has won thee, lady, and thy joys
Are placed in trifles, fashions, follies, toys,
CRABBE.

GENT,

Content, and careless of to-morrow's fare,
THOMSON.

8.
Personal Appearance of
FUTURE COMPANION.
HYACINTH.

LADY.

He is the deuce among the girls,
A thing of foppery and ton,
Of whiskers and of curls.
PIKE.

GENT.

Time from her form has ta'en away but
little of its grace.
His touch of thought hath dignified the
beauty of her face.
BAYLEY.

THE Feast of Flowers;
A Floral Game of Fortune
Boston:
Adams & Co., 25 Bromfield St.
Entered according to Act of Congress, in the
year 1869, by Adams & Co., in the Clerk's Office of
the Dist. Court, for the Dist. of Mass.

THE HAND OF FATE
Fortune Telling Game

McLoughlin Brothers
New York, N.Y., copyright 1901

The magnetic dial at the center of *The Hand of Fate* can be employed to play different games, depending upon which of the surrounding rings is used. The innermost circle allows the "hand" to answer historical questions, the middle circle provides character reading based on a player's birthday, and the outer circle, containing numbers, lets players ask true/false questions with even numbers indicating "true" and odd numbers indicating "false."

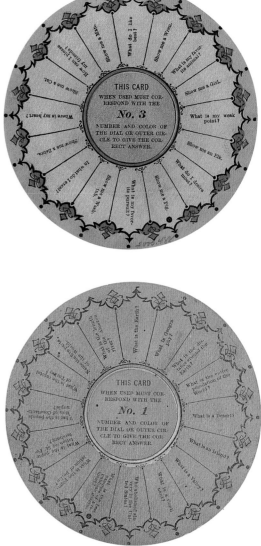

CHIROMAGICA

McLoughlin Brothers
New York, N.Y., circa 1870

McLoughlin Brothers' 1885 catalog described *Chiromagica* as a "wonderful contrivance" based on "scientific principles." The magician's hand miraculously indicates the correct answers to questions posed on the game cards.

The Giant

Nest of A.B.C.

and

Picture Blocks

❧ 2 ❧

THE WORLD'S EDUCATOR

Game manufacturers promoted their products as essential parenting tools for educating children and instilling moral values. McLoughlin Brothers' 1885 catalog claimed, "Games are a necessity in every family, and parents should see to it that their children are well supplied with them. They not only amuse, but serve to instruct and educate them. They tend to make happy firesides, and keep children at home, instead of compelling them to seek amusement away from the family circle."

A variety of games for children of all ages subtly or overtly instructed them or encouraged the development of manual skills: blocks helped coordination and taught the alphabet; puzzles developed dexterity; a whole host of quiz games encouraged memorization of historical facts; and brightly illustrated board games based on fairy tales and nursery rhymes delivered moral messages.

Many games played within the family circle reinforced subjects taught at school, such as literature, history, and geography. American board games flourished at a time when mandatory public schooling was still new and city schools were overflowing with new immigrant pupils. Game manufacturers produced enormous numbers of educational games between the 1870s and 1900s, catering to an audience sold on the notion that well-educated children provide the foundation of a moral, democratic, and prosperous nation.

PAGE 52 AND LEFT
The **GIANT NEST** *of* **A.B.C.** *and* **PICTURE BLOCKS**

MANUFACTURER UNKNOWN
UNITED STATES, CIRCA 1900

Nested blocks, consisting of a series of successively smaller hollow blocks that fit neatly one inside the other, were invented by toy manufacturer Jesse Crandall in 1881. They continue to serve as a staple of children's play today.

RIGHT
ABC BLOCKS

J. H. SINGER
NEW YORK, N.Y., CIRCA 1883

HILL'S SPELLING BLOCKS

No. 54

S.L. HILL & SON. BROOKLYN, N.Y.

HILL'S ALPHABET BLOCKS
S. L. HILL
BROOKLYN, N.Y., CIRCA 1875

Originally developed in seventeenth-century England, alphabet blocks were manufactured in New York by 1820. The first large-scale production of blocks was initiated in the Williamsburg area of Brooklyn by S. L. Hill, who patented his paper-on-wood spelling blocks in 1858.

LEFT

HILL'S SPELLING BLOCKS
S. L. HILL & SON
BROOKLYN, N.Y., 1869

Initially, spelling lessons created opportunities to impart religious knowledge. Over time, the images appearing on blocks shifted from biblical subjects to scenes and objects of everyday life, as the secular ethos superceded the religious in publicly supported schools.

ALPHABETIC OBJECT TEACHER
MANUFACTURER UNKNOWN
UNITED STATES, CIRCA 1875

CRISS CROSS SPELLING SLIPS:
Dog and Goose
MCLOUGHLIN BROTHERS
NEW YORK, N.Y., CIRCA 1890

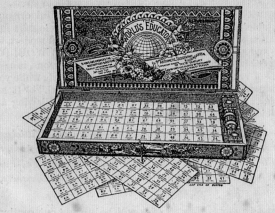

The World's Educator
OR
EDUCATIONAL GAME.
A Perfect Treasure Box, Full of Knowledge & Fun!

PATENTED IN GREAT BRITAIN
MAY 31, 1887.

PATENTED IN UNITED STATES
MAY 31, 1887.

One of the Most Wonderful Inventions OF THE 19th Century
SIMPLE IN CONSTRUCTION, ANY CHILD CAN WORK IT.

WIT, WISDOM AND WONDER.

$100 worth of Books would not give the amount of Amusement and Instruction.

THE WORLD'S EDUCATOR
W. S. REED TOY CO.
LEOMINSTER, MASS., 1887
Packaged in a beautifully lithographed wooden box, *The World's Educator* contains over two thousand quiz questions and coded answers on thirty-two large cards. Players are posed questions pertaining to history or current events, or are faced with conundrums. They then proceed to locate the correct answer on the cards using the spinning cylinder on the side of the game box.

A New DISSECTED MAP *of the* UNITED STATES

McLoughlin Brothers
New York, N.Y., copyright 1887

Children kept current with the geography of their expanding nation by completing map puzzles of the United States. Here, the area that became the state of Oklahoma in 1907 is labeled Indian Territory, and the Dakotas, which entered the Union as North and South Dakota in 1889, appear as a single territory.

CLEMENS' SILENT TEACHER: DISSECTED MAP *of the* UNITED STATES

Rev. E. J. Clemens
Clayville, N.Y., circa 1900

The imagery on this puzzle's box cover suggests that even American school children were aware of their nation's role as an international melting pot. The various national figures featured on this puzzle's box cover may represent immigrant streams; if so, then the African-American component of the population has been devalued. The black woman lacks a national costume; in fact, she wears nothing at all. The racial prejudice that pervaded Victorian society frequently found expression in the games created during this period.

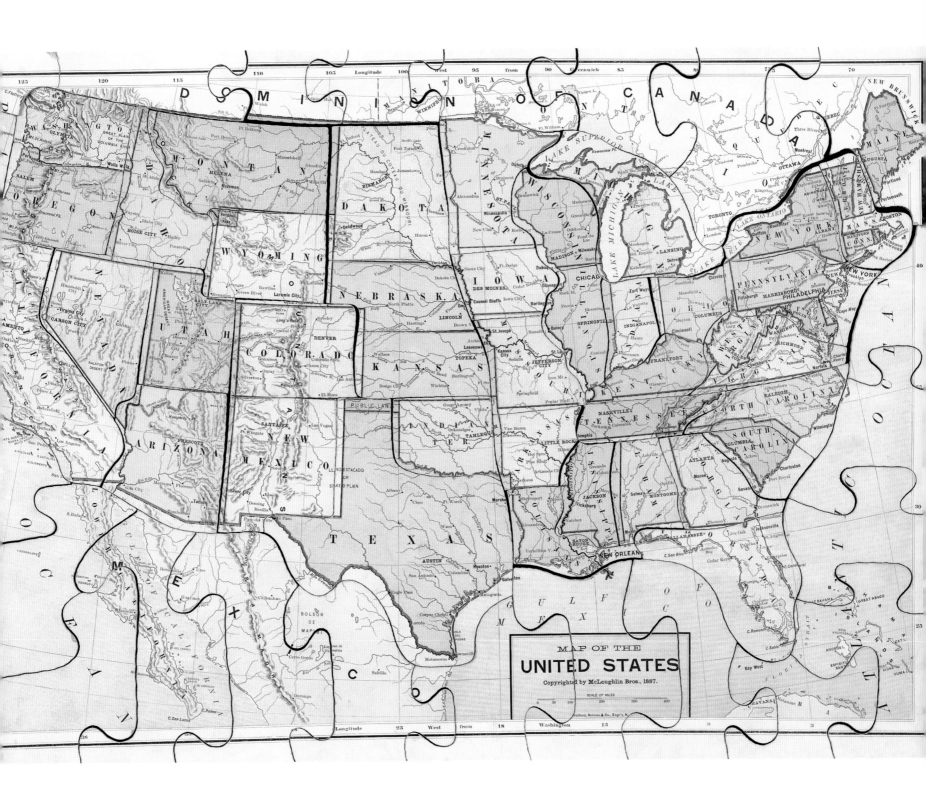

MAP OF THE
UNITED STATES
Copyrighted by McLoughlin Bros., 1887.

Improved HISTORICAL CARDS

McLoughlin Brothers
New York, N.Y., copyright 1884

YOUNG FOLKS
HISTORICAL GAME

McLoughlin Brothers
New York, N.Y., circa 1890

In the words of McLoughlin Brothers, the *Young Folks Historical Game* "affords a method by which the leading facts of American History may be fixed in the mind while indulging in a pleasant pastime." Children learn tidbits of information ranging from the date of completion of the Brooklyn Bridge to the details of significant Civil War battles.

YANKEE DOODLE: *A Game of*
AMERICAN HISTORY

Parker Brothers
Salem, Mass., copyright 1895

Players of *Yankee Doodle* compete along a pathway of American history, racing from the starting line at the Boston Tea Party (1773) to the finish line at the World's Columbian Exposition in Chicago (1893).

The HISTORISCOPE,
A PANORAMA *and*
HISTORY *of* AMERICA

Milton Bradley Co.
Springfield, Mass., circa 1875

History is livelier when viewed at the theater. The images on this scroll, which appear on a "stage," incorporate scenes from the European discovery of America to the surrender of the British at the end of the Revolution.

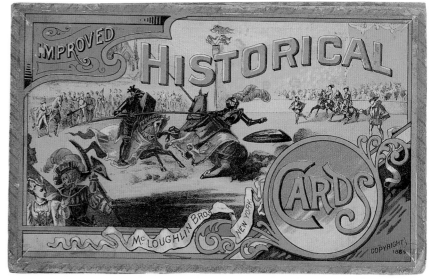

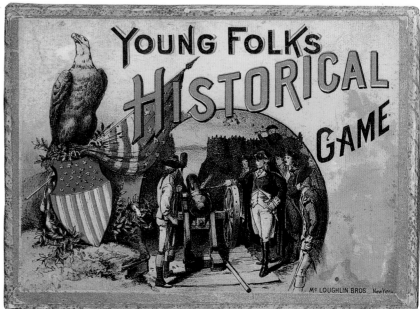

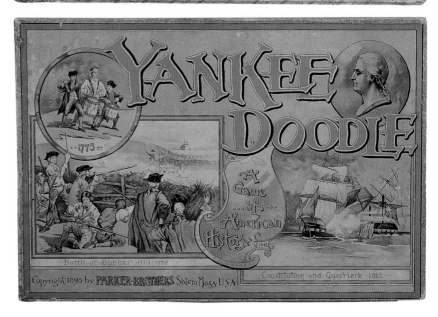

LEFT

Grandmama's
GEOGRAPHICAL GAME
McLoughlin Brothers
New York, N.Y., copyright 1900

RIGHT

Grandmama's Sunday Game of
BIBLE QUESTIONS: *New Testament*
McLoughlin Brothers
New York, N.Y., copyright 1887

FAR RIGHT

Grandmama's Improved Game of
USEFUL KNOWLEDGE
McLoughlin Brothers
New York, N.Y., copyright 1887

McLoughlin Brothers introduced the successful "Grandmama's" series of educational card games in 1887. In the *Game of Useful Knowledge*, players assume the role of "scholars" and designate one participant to act as "preceptor." Scholars test their knowledge by answering questions posed on cards, and the preceptor confirms or corrects them after consulting the companion book of answers.

51.

What causes day?

The shining of the sun on the earth.

5.

What is wind?

The air put in motion, and supposed to be caused by its rushing from a colder to a hotter place.

15.

What are hams?

The legs of hogs, salted and dried.

AUTOGRAPH AUTHORS

McLoughlin Brothers
New York, N.Y., copyright 1886

The game of *Authors*, produced in a multiplicity of versions, was one of the best-selling educational card games of the late-nineteenth century. Players build "suits" of cards composed of authors and their major works. The stars of *Autograph Authors* are the famous writers of the time, including Mark Twain (who appears on the cover), James Fennimore Cooper, James Russell Lowell, and William Cullen Bryant.

Game of
MUSICAL AUTHORS

McLoughlin Brothers
New York, N.Y., copyright 1882

A variation on the more popular *Authors* game, *Musical Authors* familiarizes players with famous composers—such as Handel, Beethoven, Chopin, and Wagner—and their major works.

The Game of
MYTHOLOGY

Peter G. Thomson
Cincinnati, Ohio, copyright 1884

RIGHT
GEMS *of* ART

Selchow & Righter
New York, N.Y., copyright 1880

GEMS OF ART

ANEW INSTRUCTIVE AND ENTERTAINING GAME

FIVE ENTIRELY NEW GAMES CAN BE PLAYED WITH THESE CARDS

PUBLISHED BY
SELCHOW & RIGHTER, N.Y.

COPYRIGHT 1880 BY C.G.HARGER, JR.

The course of true love
never did run smooth.

In maiden meditation fancy
free.

A fine frenzy.

Midsummer Night's Dream.

In single blessedness.

Confusion worse con-
founded.

That bad eminence.

A pillar of state.

Milton.

Human face divine.

The noblest Roman of
them all.

Play of Julius Cæsar.

The dogs of war.

The most unkindest cut of all.

Not tnat I loved Cæsar less
but Rome more.

Where ignorance is bliss,
'tis folly to be wise.

Gray.

The short and simple annals of
the poor.

The paths of glory lead but to
the grave.

A youth to fortune and to fame
unknown.

The New Game of
FAMILIAR QUOTATIONS
McLoughlin Brothers
New York, N.Y., copyright 1887
As in the popular game of *Authors*,
players of *Familiar Quotations* attempt
to build complete suits composed of
five quotations from a single author.
In the process, players learn to identify
the words of famous authors, from
William Shakespeare to Benjamin
Franklin.

THE NEW GAME

FAMILIAR QUOTATIONS

FROM

POPULAR AUTHORS.

McLoughlin Bros.   COPYRIGHTED 1887   New York.

LITTLE GOLDENLOCKS
and the **THREE BEARS:**
A Pleasing Game
McLoughlin Brothers
New York, N.Y., copyright 1890

LITTLE RED RIDING HOOD
McLoughlin Brothers
New York, N.Y., circa 1890

JACK *the* GIANT KILLER

McLoughlin Brothers
New York, N.Y., copyright 1890

Games based on fairy tales and nursery rhymes were a popular form of entertainment with the youngest of board game players. *Jack the Giant Killer* is based on the classic fairy tale set in the time of King Arthur, when fearsome giants roamed the land. The idea of a little man defeating a big one was popular in a post-colonial nation committed to championing the underdog.

LITTLE RED RIDING HOOD

McLOUGHLIN BROS. N.Y.

LEFT
LITTLE RED RIDING HOOD
McLoughlin Brothers
New York, N.Y., circa 1885

RIGHT
Game of
BA-A, BA-A, BLACK SHEEP
McLoughlin Brothers
New York, N.Y., copyright 1888

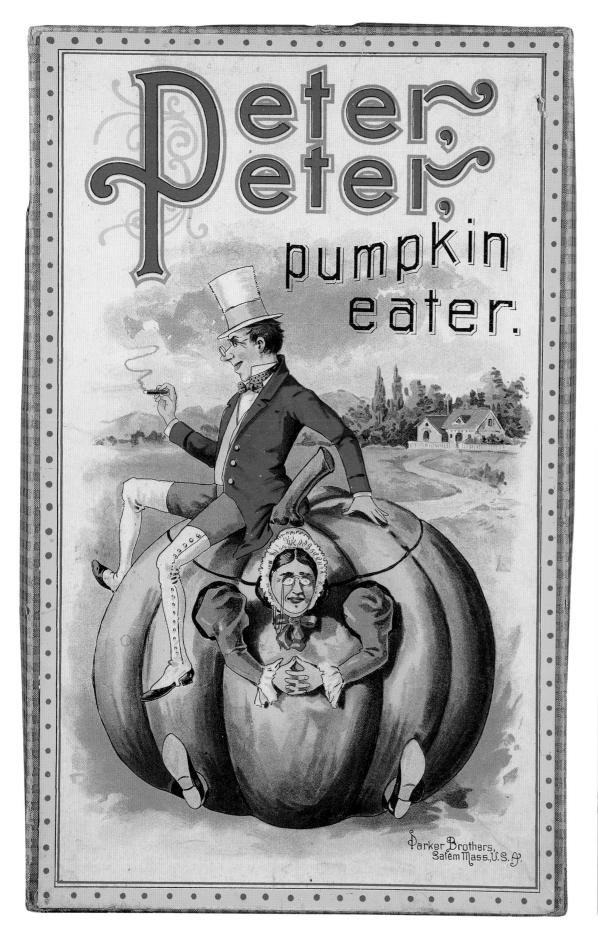

❊ 3 ❊

MORALS
TO
MATERIALISM

Board games provide a fascinating illustration of changing attitudes toward success in late-nineteenth-century America. The earliest games made in the United States were based on a model of success defined by virtuous Christian living. In one of the earliest American board games, *Mansion of Happiness* (1843), players advance by landing on spaces denoting virtues such as piety, honesty, and humility, and lose ground when landing on vices such as cruelty, immodesty, and ingratitude. The wildly popular *Checkered Game of Life* (1860), in which players follow a checkerboard path through the stages of life, similarly advances players for observing moral behavior, although significantly introduces the accumulation of points as the player's ultimate goal.

A new type of board game emerged in the 1880s, a decade of economic expansion and optimism. Materialism rather than morality became the focus of games, with players achieving success through competitive, capitalist behavior. In the *Game of District Messenger Boy* (1886), for instance, players rise through the ranks from gofer to president of the firm. Although morality games did not completely disappear (*Mansion of Happiness*, for example, was revived in the 1890s), games encouraging the competitive American spirit dominated the marketplace, eventually giving rise to the perennial favorite *Monopoly* (1935).

PAGE 76
The CHECKERED *Game of* LIFE
MILTON BRADLEY CO.
SPRINGFIELD, MASS., 1866
The marriage of spiritual values and worldly achievement first appeared in Milton Bradley's inaugural game, *The Checkered Game of Life*. As in *The Mansion of Happiness*, the game taught the lesson of success achieved through virtuous living; Bradley's game, however, also secularized the notion of virtuous living by rewarding material accomplishments. Players travel through life, represented by a checkerboard, in pursuit of success—defined here as the accumulation of one hundred points and the attainment of happy old age.

RIGHT
The MANSION *of* HAPPINESS
MCLOUGHLIN BROTHERS
NEW YORK, N.Y., COPYRIGHT 1895
This 1895 "modernized" version of one of America's earliest board games maintains the simple moralistic themes of its predecessor, updated with larger, more luxurious packaging. The player's goal, the "Mansion of Happiness," evolved from an image of a peaceful, Christian heaven in 1843 to this game's opulent Taj Mahal.

FAR RIGHT
The MANSION *of* HAPPINESS
W. & S. B. IVES AND E. B. SELCHOW & CO.
SALEM, MASS., AND NEW YORK, N.Y., 1864
In this earliest of American board games, players strive to occupy the Seat of Happiness at the center of the board by living a virtuous life. Based on the Puritan view that success is achieved through Christian deeds and goodness, games such as this reflect the dominant beliefs of pre–Civil War America.

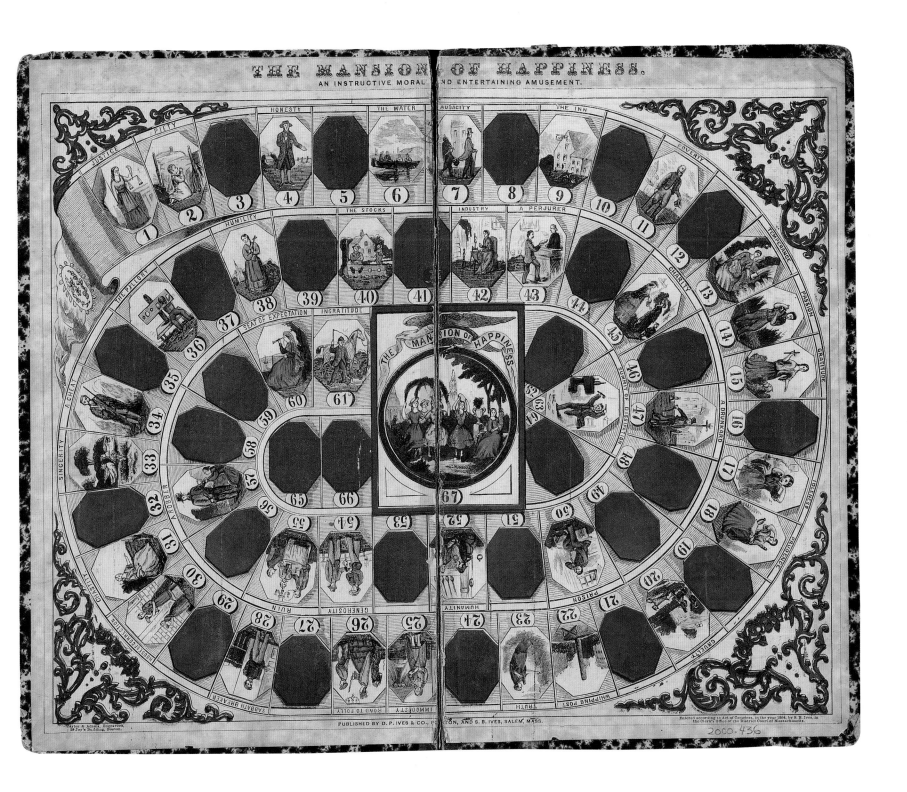

The New
PILGRIM'S PROGRESS

McLoughlin Brothers
New York, N.Y., copyright 1893

Based on John Bunyan's timeless classic published in 1678, *Pilgrim's Progress* leads players along a multi-colored path from the City of Destruction to the Celestial City. Still in production and popular in the Christian game market today, the game of *Pilgrim's Progress* continues to inculcate religious values in American "pilgrims."

THE CELESTIAL CITY

THE RIVER OF DEATH

BEULAH LAND

DOUBTING CASTLE OF GIANT DESPAIR

WAIT OVER FOUR TURNS

WAIT FOR A ONE TO CROSS OVER

SLEEP OVER ONE TURN

ARBOR IN ENCHANTED LAND

Go Forward THREE

Go Forward FOUR

Go Forward FIVE

THE DELECTABLE MOUNTAINS

VANITY FAIR

THE FLATTERERS NET

TO FLATTERERS NET

FAITHFUL BURNED

THE VALLEY OF THE SHADOW OF DEATH

WAIT OVER ONE TURN

Castle

SEVENTH THROW GOES TO CELESTIAL CITY

Wait over Two Turns

Begin over

APOLLYON

LIFE

Begin over

Victorious go forward four

Conquered begin over

ARBOR

Go Back to ARBOR

THE HOUSE BEAUTIFUL

Go Forward Five

Valley of Humiliation

Hill of Difficulty

ARBOR

THE CROSS

MT. SINAI

CITY OF DESTRUCTION

STOP HERE ON EXACT THROW

INTERPRETERS HOUSE

THE WICKET GATE

BACK TO PATH

Go Forward to THE CROSS

Go Forward to THE CROSS

TO SINAI

SLOUGH OF DESPOND

WAIT OVER ONE TURN

BULLS AND BEARS:
The Great Wall St. Game
McLOUGHLIN BROTHERS
NEW YORK, N.Y., PATENTED 1883

By the 1880s, wealth had emerged as the defining characteristic of success in American games, as in life. *Bulls and Bears* was based on the vicissitudes of the stock market—an ideal theme for games— and was designed to make players feel like speculators, bankers, and brokers, if only for a time. Possibly illustrated by famed political cartoonist Thomas Nast, who provided illustrations for some of McLoughlin Brothers' books, the gameboard depicts a nattily dressed bull and bear shearing sheep (under the removable spinner), a subtle commentary on the making of financial empires at the public's expense.

Bulls and Bears is unusual among nineteenth-century board games in incorporating caricatures of contemporary figures. In the lower corners of the board (opposite page), railroad magnates William Henry Vanderbilt and Jay Gould, whose speculations contributed to the financial panic that inspired this game, smugly read ticker tape showing the value of their stock. Gould is also shown at the top left looking glum as he contemplates the bear market. Cyrus Field, a railroad investor in collaboration with Gould, appears opposite him armed to defend his money bags.

THE MODERN COLOSSUS OF (RAIL) ROADS.

JOSEPH KEPPLER
The Modern Colossus of (Rail) Roads
CARTOON, PUBLISHED IN *PUCK*
DECEMBER 10, 1879

The caricatures of William Henry Vanderbilt, Jay Gould, and Cyrus W. Field that embellish the corners of the *Bulls and Bears* gameboard bear a striking resemblance to those lampooning the capitalists in Joseph Keppler's political cartoon "The Modern Colossus of (Rail) Roads," which appeared in the weekly illustrated magazine *Puck* in 1879. Keppler's scathing depiction of Vanderbilt holding the reins of the railroads with cohorts Field and Gould attacks railroad monopolies that snuffed competition and hiked freight prices.

"Modern Colossus" alludes to the Statue of Liberty, which in 1879 was only partially completed, the arm and torch standing sentinel in New York's Madison Square Park to lure potential donors to fund the building of the statue's base. Lady Liberty earned the epithet "Modern Colossus" because of the ancient bronze statue that inspired her, the *Colossus of Rhodes*—"Roads" in Keppler's cartoon.

Games of
MONOPOLIST, MARINER'S COMPASS, *and* **TEN UP**
McLoughlin Brothers
New York, N.Y., circa 1885
The advertisement for *Monopolist* in the McLoughlin Brothers' 1885 catalog reads: "On this board the great struggle between Capital and Labor can be fought out to the satisfaction of all parties, and, if the players are successful, they can break the Monopolist and become Monopolists themselves."

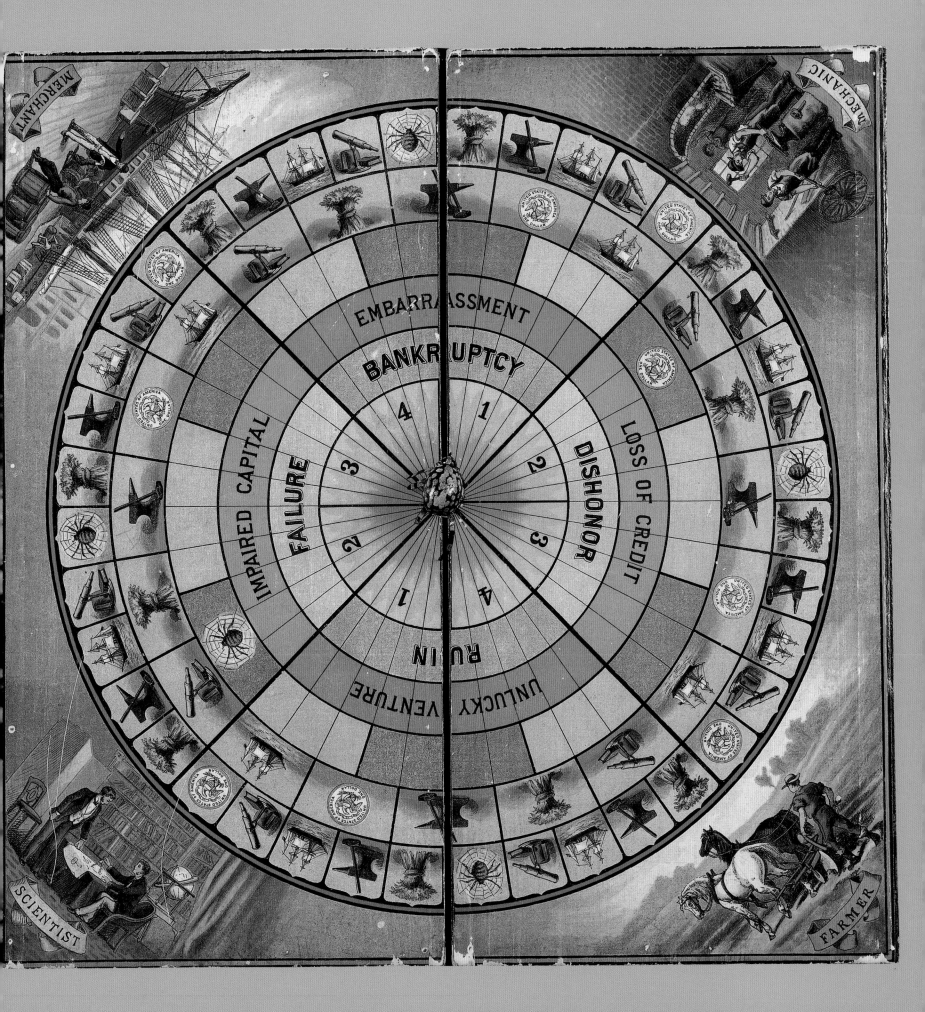

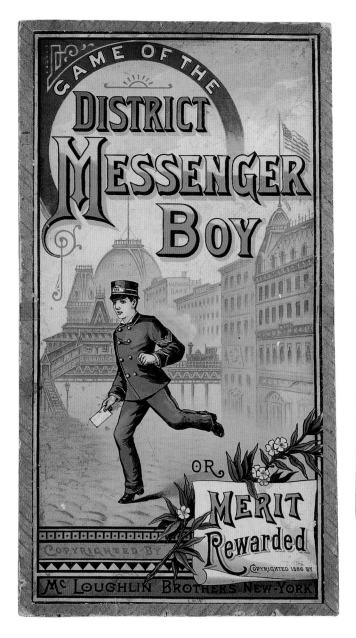

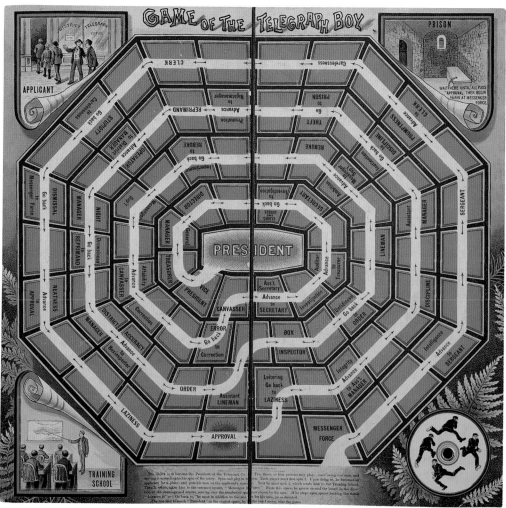

ABOVE AND BOTTOM RIGHT

Game of the
DISTRICT MESSENGER BOY,
or MERIT REWARDED

MCLOUGHLIN BROTHERS
NEW YORK, N.Y., COPYRIGHT 1886

One of many games produced in the 1880s with a "rags to riches" theme, *The District Messenger Boy* reflects the contemporary belief that the American capitalist system would reward merit and enterprise regardless of one's background, privileged or humble. Players start the game as messenger boys and attempt to work their way up through the ranks to become president of the firm.

ABOVE

The Game of
TELEGRAPH BOY,
or MERIT REWARDED

MCLOUGHLIN BROTHERS
NEW YORK, N.Y., COPYRIGHT 1888

Introduced into the popular imagination by the novels of Horatio Alger, the American dream is played out in this McLoughlin Brothers' spin-off of the *Game of District Messenger Boy*.

FAR RIGHT

The Game of
DISTRICT MESSENGER BOY

MCLOUGHLIN BROTHERS
NEW YORK, N.Y., CIRCA 1888

CASH: HONESTY
is the Best **POLICY**

J. H. Singer
New York, N.Y., circa 1890

Cash provided those who could afford the
simple $1.50 game with the opportunity to climb
the ladder from errand boy to millionaire.

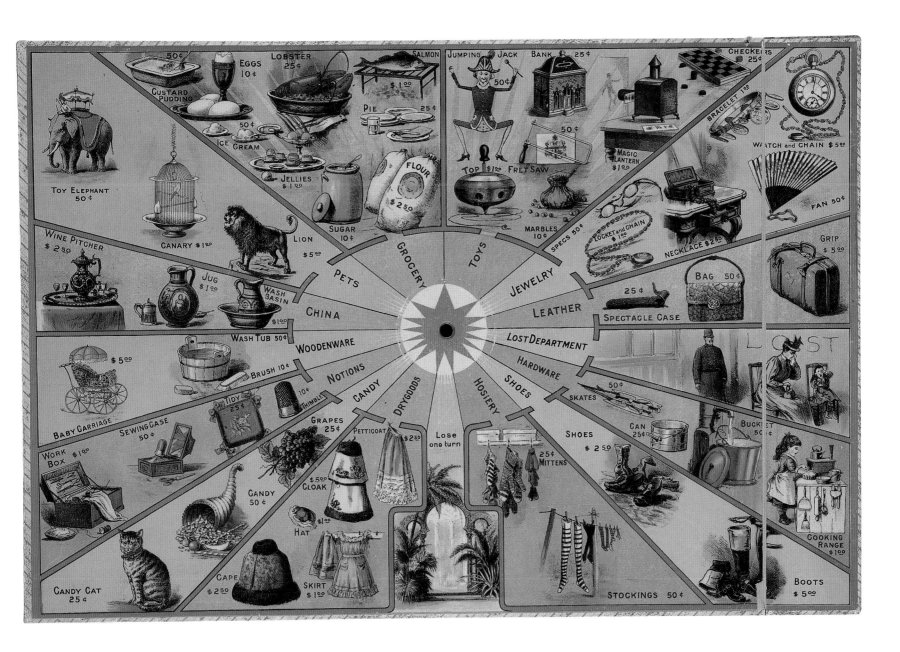

The Game of
PLAYING DEPARTMENT STORE

MᴄLᴏᴜɢʜʟɪɴ Bʀᴏᴛʜᴇʀs
Nᴇᴡ Yᴏʀᴋ, N.Y., ᴄᴏᴘʏʀɪɢʜᴛ 1898

Inspired by a recent American innovation—
shopping emporiums selling a wide variety of
goods under one roof—this game encouraged
players to accumulate the greatest quantity of
goods while spending their money as wisely
as possible.

WHEAT

100

WHEAT

PIT: EXCITING FUN *for* EVERYONE

PARKER BROTHERS
SALEM, MASS., 1919

Introduced in 1904, the lively trading game *Pit* simulates the ups and downs, desperate deals, and nonstop action of an actual trading floor. Just as traders of important commodities such as cotton and gold made and lost fortunes competing in the capital of capitalism, New York, players of *Pit* win and lose hands in a frenetic attempt to corner a commodity on the American Corn Exchange.

ABOVE AND RIGHT

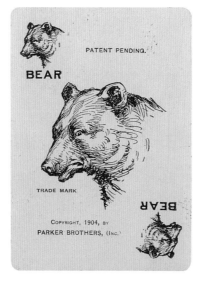

PATENT PENDING.

BEAR

TRADE MARK

BEAR

COPYRIGHT, 1904, BY
PARKER BROTHERS, (INC.)

OATS

60

OATS

PORK

PORK

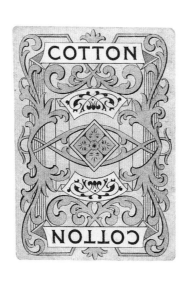

COTTON

COTTON

COFFEE

COFFEE

LEFT AND RIGHT

COMMERCE

J. OTTMAN LITH. CO.
NEW YORK, N.Y., CIRCA 1900

In the card game *Commerce*, players attempt to collect all of the cards of a certain commodity by yelling bids to other players. In their frenzied efforts to corner the market, players do not take turns but rather win their cards by out-yelling their opponents.

4

WAR GAMES

The appropriateness of war games, especially for children, is much debated today. In earlier times, however, such pastimes were freely and guiltlessly enjoyed by family members of all ages. American fascination with current events found expression in numerous board games representing military conflict, from the nation's Civil War (1861–65) to the Franco-Prussian War (1870–71) in Europe. The Spanish-American War (1898), from which the United States emerged as an aggressive new international power, inspired games reflecting patriotic pride in the country's naval victory over Spain and admiration for the military exploits of Theodore Roosevelt and his Rough Riders.

Some game manufacturers also catered directly to the needs of American servicemen. During the Civil War, for instance, Milton Bradley distributed a compendium of games to Union troops. Compact enough to fit into a knapsack, the kit included *The Checkered Game of Life* along with chess, checkers, and dominoes.

PAGE 92
The Great Game:
UNCLE SAM AT WAR WITH SPAIN
RHODE ISLAND GAME CO.
PROVIDENCE, R.I., COPYRIGHT 1898
The manufacturer's encouragement to players to "let the Americans show what they would have done had they been on Spanish war vessels" reflects the intense pride that Americans felt after their victory in the Spanish-American War. Like other games attuned to the war theme, *Uncle Sam at War with Spain* appealed to young boys, whose patriotic fervor was stirred by incendiary headlines and pictorial supplements in the tabloid newspapers.

LEFT AND RIGHT
Game of **WAR AT SEA**
or "Don't Give Up the Ship"
McLOUGHLIN BROTHERS
NEW YORK, N.Y., COPYRIGHT 1898
Although the subtitle of this game recalls the famous words of War of 1812 hero Captain James Lawrence, *War at Sea* was inspired by the United States' naval victories in the Spanish-American War of some eighty years later. The object of the game is to see which fleet can sweep the sea clear of the other.

Game of
NAPOLEON:
THE LITTLE CORPORAL

PARKER BROTHERS
SALEM, MASS., COPYRIGHT 1895

Napoleon Bonaparte's legendary conquests of the
early nineteenth century continued to captivate the
American imagination long after the French ruler's
downfall. *The Game of Napoleon* leads players
through the life of Napoleon, from his early
military victories, to his coronation as emperor,
to his final exile on St. Helena.

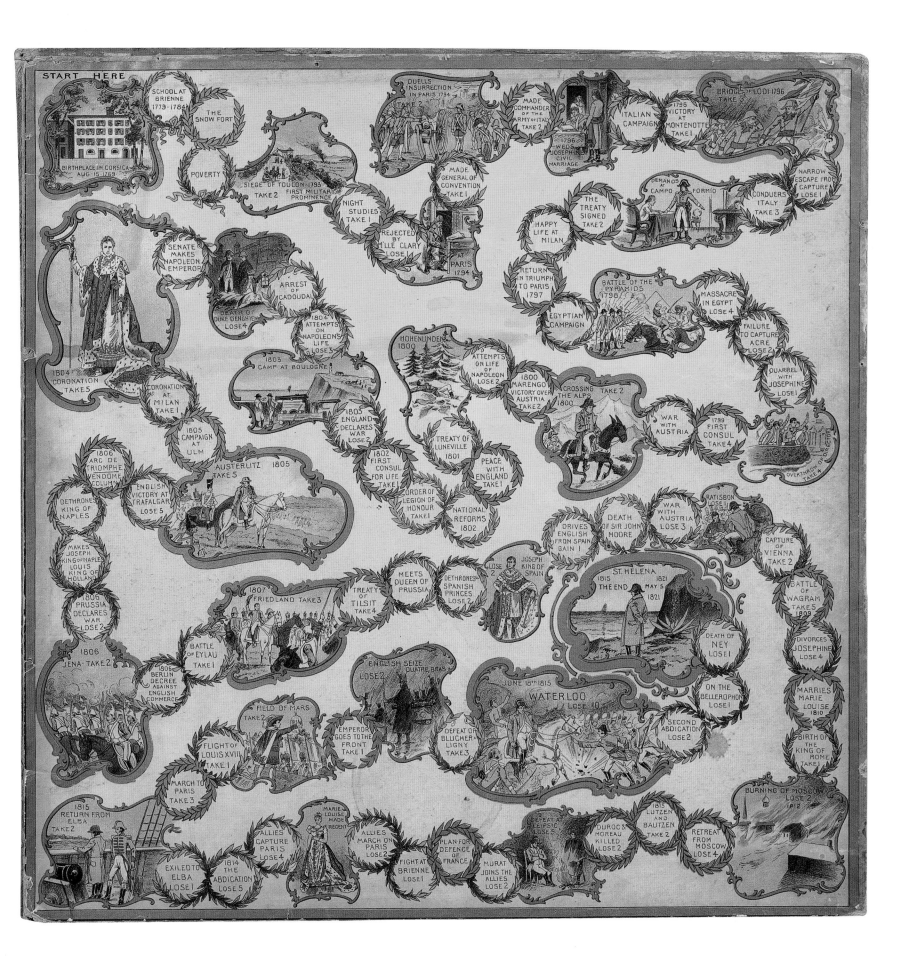

ABOVE AND RIGHT
ADVANCE *and* **RETREAT:**
A Game of Skill
MCLOUGHLIN BROTHERS
NEW YORK, N.Y., COPYRIGHT 1900

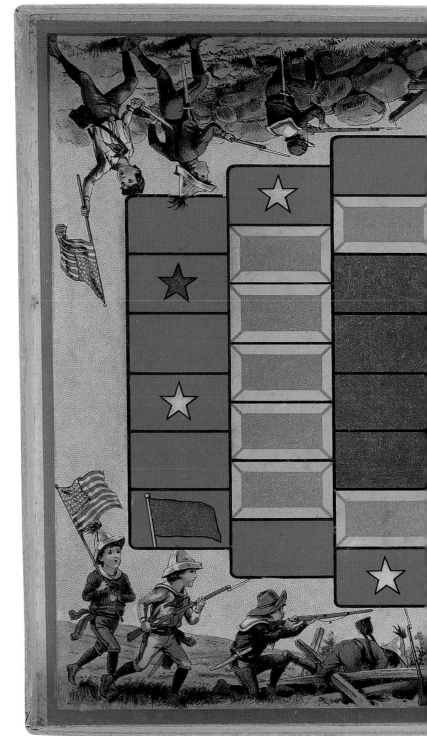

ABOVE
Game of The
LITTLE VOLUNTEER
MCLOUGHLIN BROTHERS
NEW YORK, N.Y., COPYRIGHT 1898
The object of this game is "to see which little
Volunteer can rise from the ranks to be
Commander-in-Chief." Grisly images showing
bloodshed were apparently not troubling
to children and parents of the 1890s.

RIGHT
ROOSEVELT AT SAN JUAN
CHAFFEE & SELCHOW
NEW YORK, N.Y., COPYRIGHT 1899

ABOVE
SCHLEY AT SANTIAGO BAY
CHAFFEE & SELCHOW
NEW YORK, N.Y., COPYRIGHT 1899

From a series of patriotic games inspired by the
Spanish-American War, *Schley at Santiago Bay*
celebrates war hero Winfield Scott Schley while
teaching players facts about the recent war. Schley,
hardly a household name today, was the U.S.
Navy commodore in command of the Flying
Squadron during the victorious battle of Santiago.
An investigation conducted two years after the
publication of this game found Schley guilty of
negligence and misconduct during the battle.

STARRY FLAG SERIES.   COPYRIGHT 1899, BY CHAFFEE & SELCHOW, NEW YORK.

---

2   H   D

What should New York City thank Roosevelt for?

What does Roosevelt think should be the aim of American statesmen?

ANSWER·

To hasten the day when no European will have a foothold in America.

Name standard work that Roosevelt has written?

How does Roosevelt regard politics and war?

---

5   C

Where did the Rough Riders land in Cuba?

Why was Santiago selected as a point of attack?

ANSWER:

The Spanish fleet lay in the harbor, which was mined, and our ships could not enter.

What fact rendered the attack on Santiago very peculiar?

From what point did the Rough Riders set sail?

---

3   B

What office did Roosevelt hold at the opening of the war?

What maxim of Washington did Roosevelt quote a year before the war?

ANSWER:

To be prepared for war is the most effectual means to promote peace.

What prediction did Roosevelt make before the Maine was blown up?

How did Roosevelt prepare for the expected war?

PAGES 102–03 AND ABOVE
ROUGH RIDER TEN-PINS
R. BLISS MANUFACTURING CO.
PAWTUCKET, R.I., CIRCA 1898

"Rough Riders" was the popular name for the
1st Regiment of the U.S. Cavalry Volunteers,
organized largely by Theodore Roosevelt during
the Spanish-American War. Its members were
mostly ranchers and cowboys from the West,
with a sprinkling of adventurous blue bloods
from eastern universities. The "pins" in this
bowling game represent cowgirls, Rough
Riders, Indians, Mexicans, and "cowboy dudes."

RIGHT
MIMIC WAR
EDGAR O. CLARK
NEW YORK, N.Y., CIRCA 1898

In *Mimic War*, thirty military figures are used
by children to act out their favorite war battles.
Though the box cover illustrates soldiers
from the Franco-Prussian War, the "action"
figures inside are dressed in the naval
and military costume of the more recent
Spanish-American War.

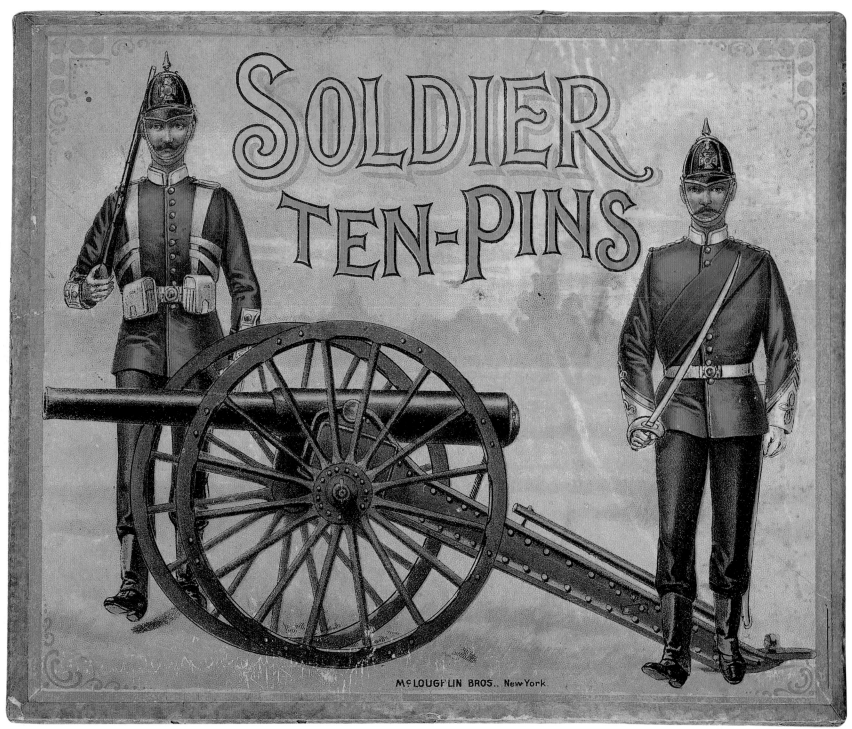

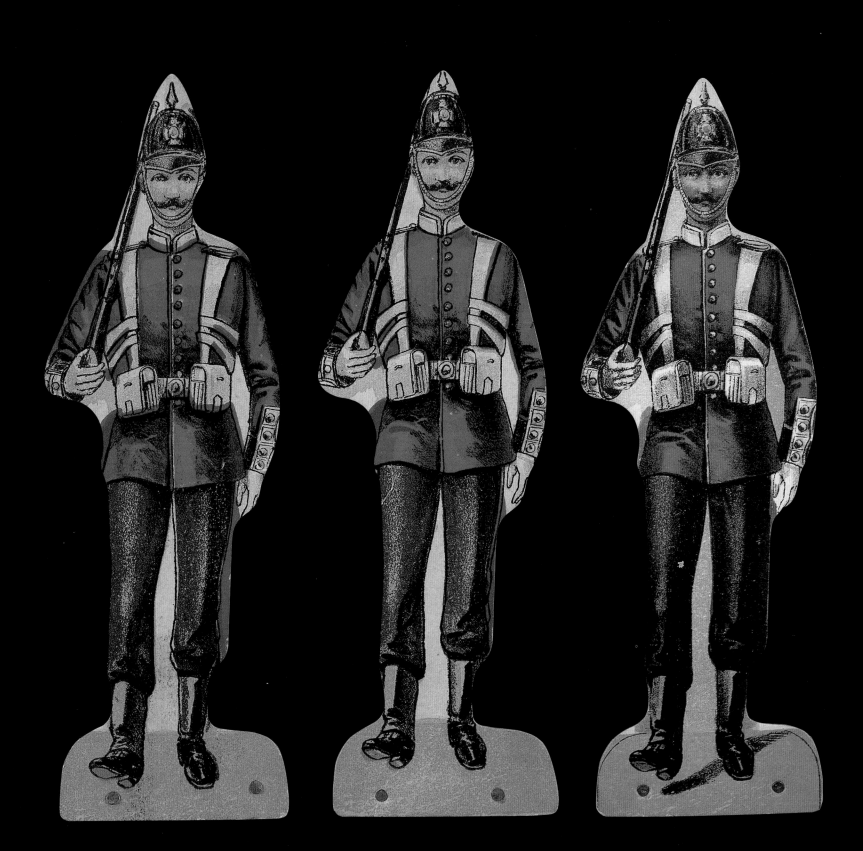

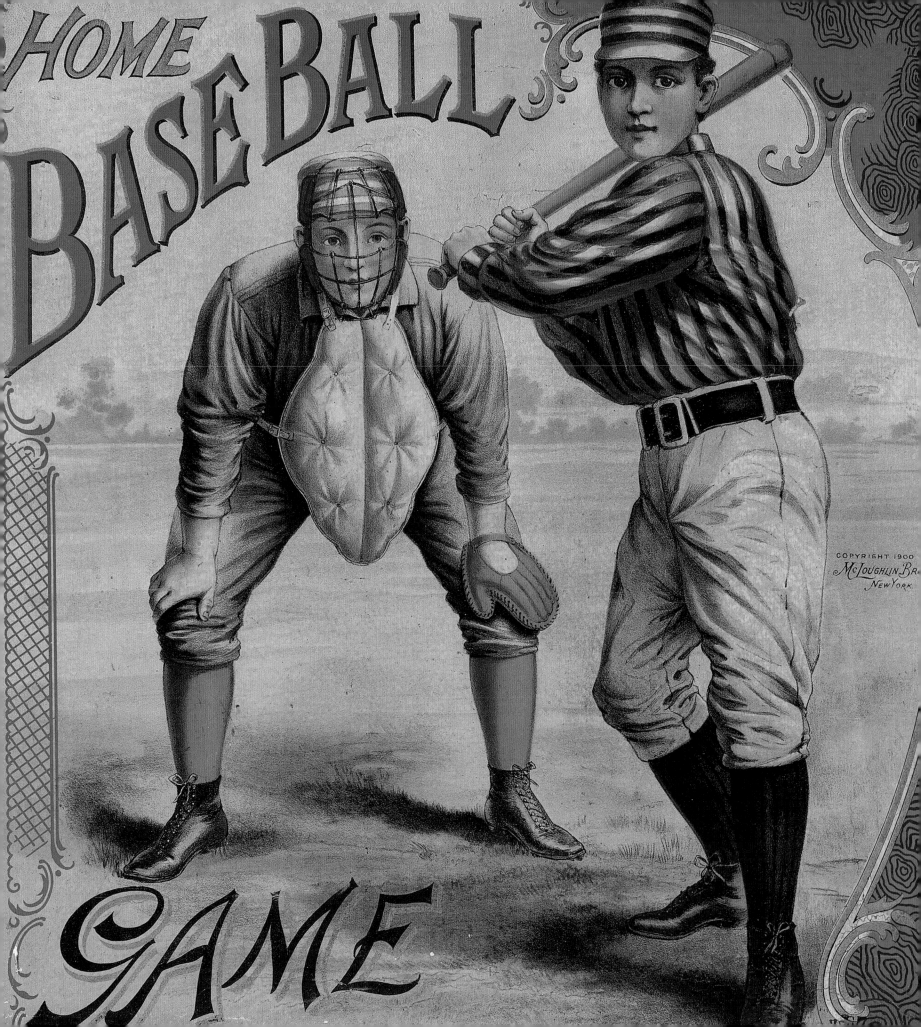

5

PARLOR
ATHLETICS

During the late-nineteenth century, Americans developed an infatuation with organized competitive sports, participating and observing as never before. Middle-class Americans joined athletic clubs, competed in team sports, and cheered on players at sporting events. These activities were encouraged by social reformers, who maintained that athletics contributed to individual health, morality, and character and to the greater benefit of society. Board game manufacturers rode the wave of popularity, producing an endless variety of family games centered around baseball, basketball, football, and golf. Baseball, a distinctly American sport and national pastime, appeared as a board game subject by the 1860s. The excitement of racing sports—particularly those involving horses, bicycles, and boats—could be enjoyed indoors, in miniature, with players racing around a game board.

While some late-nineteenth century parlor games imitate true athletic endeavors, others challenged players' own physical skill and dexterity. *Fish Pond*, one of childhood's most enduring dexterity games, requires players to hook colorful cardboard fish out of a stocked "pond" using wooden fishing rods. Adult skill and action games included *Pillow Dex*, a forerunner of Ping-Pong, in which players volleyed a balloon over a net stretched across a table.

PAGE 108
HOME BASEBALL
MCLOUGHLIN BROTHERS
NEW YORK, N.Y., COPYRIGHT 1900
The popular sport of baseball inspired numerous board games that transformed spectators into players. McLoughlin Brothers promoted *Home Baseball* as "a perfect counterpart of Base-ball in the open air. Base-ball during inclement weather, and the long winter evenings, can be transferred to the home circle, and there it will prove doubly attractive, because both ladies and gentlemen can compete on equal terms."

RIGHT, TOP
Game of BASE-BALL
MCLOUGHLIN BROTHERS
NEW YORK, N.Y., COPYRIGHT 1886
The quantity and variety of baseball board games that survive from the late-nineteenth century signal a long-standing passion for the nation's favorite sport. *Game of Base-ball* includes painted metal game pieces in the form of baseball players.

RIGHT, BOTTOM
The Game of BASKETBALL
CHAFFEE & SELCHOW AND MCLOUGHLIN BROTHERS
NEW YORK, N.Y., COPYRIGHT 1898
Women's basketball was introduced on the Northampton, Massachusetts, campus of Smith College in 1892, less than one year after the game's invention. By 1898, when this game appeared, women were playing basketball at recreation centers, YWCAs, college gymnasiums, settlement houses, and high schools across the country.

Game of GOLF

McLoughlin Brothers
New York, N.Y., copyright 1896

Golf was one of only a few sports enjoyed by both men and women at the end of the nineteenth century. *Game of Golf* references the sport in its illustrations but is essentially a simple race game in which players vie to be the first to reach the opposite end of the golf course, passing the clubhouse en route to the finish line.

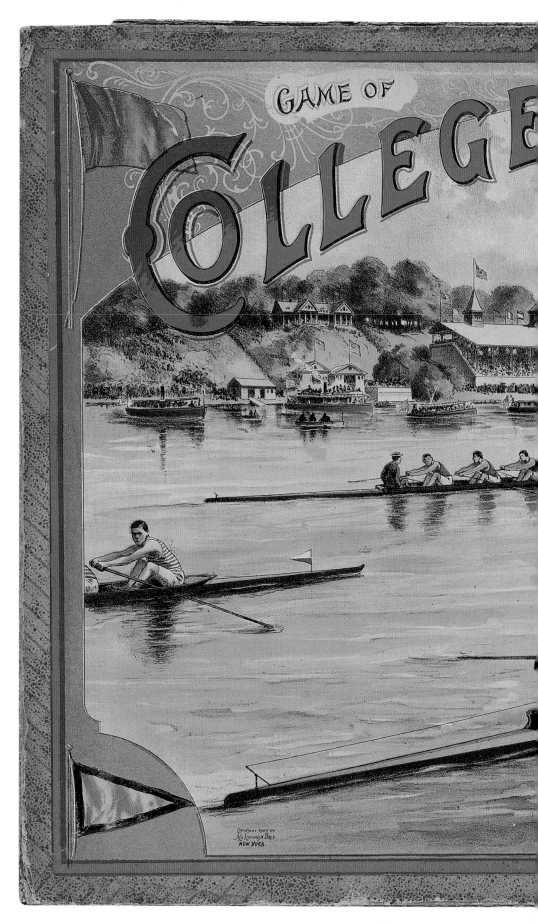

Game of
COLLEGE BOAT RACE
MᴄLᴏᴜɢʜʟɪɴ Bʀᴏᴛʜᴇʀs
Nᴇᴡ Yᴏʀᴋ, N.Y., ᴄᴏᴘʏʀɪɢʜᴛ 1900

BOAT RACE

Mc LOUGHLIN BROS.
NEW YORK.

Game of
BICYCLE RACE

McLoughlin Brothers
New York, N.Y., copyright 1891

Popular in the 1880s, the sport of bicycling had
evolved into a national obsession by the 1890s.
Unlike today, bicycling was primarily a group
activity rather than a solitary pursuit. In this
1891 version of the *Game of Bicycle Race* players
representing regional bicycle clubs (New York,
Boston, Philadelphia, and Chicago) compete to
be the first around a race track.

Game of
BICYCLE RACE

McLoughlin Brothers
New York, N.Y., copyright 1895

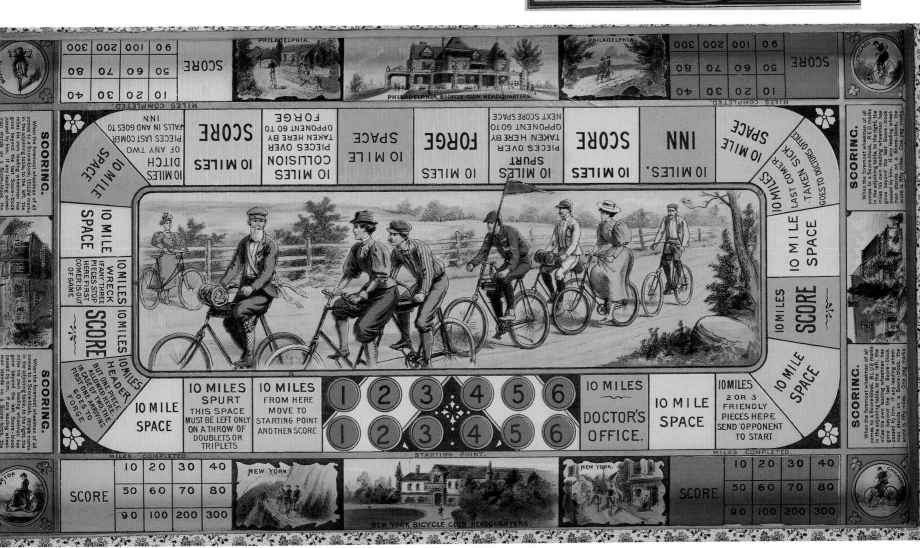

FASCINATION

Published by SELCHOW & RIGHTER N.Y.

FASCINATION

Selchow & Righter
New York, N.Y., circa 1890

Game of
RING TOSS

R. Bliss Manufacturing Co.
Pawtucket, R.I., circa 1890

PIGS IN CLOVER

Selchow & Righter
New York, N.Y., circa 1880

The first popular dexterity game in America, *Pigs in Clover* challenges players to manipulate marbles (pigs) into the central circle (the pigpen) by carefully rotating and tilting the game. Games such as this reflect the theories of educators such as Friedrich Froebel, Maria Montessori, and John Dewey, who promoted practical experience and manual skills as a key component of childhood education.

These people are having great Fun! They are playing the laughable, exciting, new game of "Pillow Dex."

FOR ANY NUMBER OF PLAYERS.

HOW TO PLAY THE GAME.

Inflate one of the balloons.

Divide the players into two teams, sitting opposite sides of the table, down which a line is drawn (see illustration on cover.)

THE IDEA is to keep the "Pillow Dex" balloon, which is struck lightly to and fro, from landing on your side of the line.

Make it land on your opponent's side of the line, if you can, for when it does so, it counts you a point.

The side getting ten points first WINS THE GAME.

EXTRA "PILLOW DEX" balloons will be mailed, postpaid, by the Publishers, Parker Bros., Salem, Mass., 6 for 25 cents; 12 for 50 cents.

We prefer to have you send money-order, but we will accept postage stamps.

LEFT AND RIGHT, TOP
PILLOW DEX
PARKER BROTHERS
SALEM, MASS., COPYRIGHT 1896

In *Pillow Dex*, a precursor of *Ping-Pong*, players volley a balloon over a net stretched across the parlor table. Introduced by Parker Brothers in the 1890s, *Pillow Dex* was one of the most heavily advertised games of the period.

RIGHT, BOTTOM
PILLOW DEX TENNIS
PARKER BROTHERS
SALEM, MASS., COPYRIGHT 1897

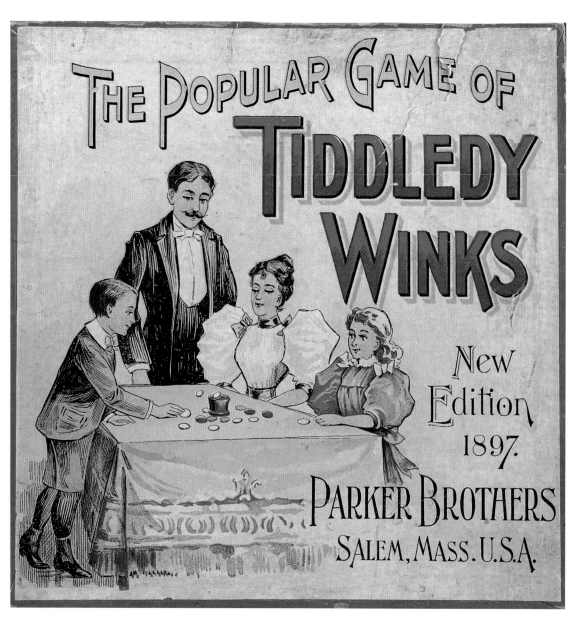

LEFT
The Popular Game of
TIDDLEDY WINKS
PARKER BROTHERS
SALEM, MASS., COPYRIGHT 1897

RIGHT
Improved Game of
TIDDLEDY WINKS
McLOUGHLIN BROTHERS
NEW YORK, N.Y., PATENTED 1890

Tiddledy Winks, first patented in England in 1889 and marketed to an adult audience, captivated Americans during the 1890s. Players attempt to send a game piece (wink) flying into the air using another instrument (tiddledy, or squidger) and make it land in a cup. The player placing the most winks in the cup wins the game. The modern spelling, "tiddlywinks," came into use during the 1950s.

COMBINATION
TIDDLEDY WINKS
McLoughlin Brothers
New York, N.Y., circa 1890

The New Game of
KING'S QUOITS
McLoughlin Brothers
New York, N.Y., copyright 1893

The New Game of King's Quoits is a variation of *Tiddledy Winks* in which players try to ring pegs by jumping donut-shaped bone disks off a mat.

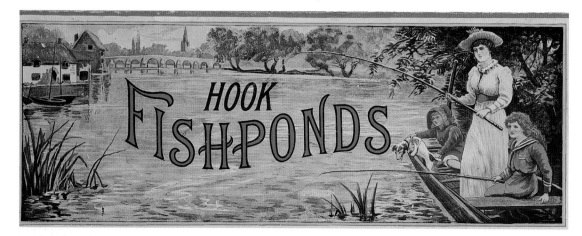

LEFT, TOP
The Game of
FISH POND
MᴄLᴏᴜɢʜʟɪɴ Bʀᴏᴛʜᴇʀs
Nᴇᴡ Yᴏʀᴋ, N.Y., ᴄɪʀᴄᴀ 1890

LEFT, CENTER
HOOK FISHPONDS
Mᴀɴᴜғᴀᴄᴛᴜʀᴇʀ ᴜɴᴋɴᴏᴡɴ
Uɴɪᴛᴇᴅ Sᴛᴀᴛᴇs, ᴄɪʀᴄᴀ 1890

LEFT, BOTTOM
FISH POND:
A Popular Game
MᴄLᴏᴜɢʜʟɪɴ Bʀᴏᴛʜᴇʀs
Nᴇᴡ Yᴏʀᴋ, N.Y., ᴄɪʀᴄᴀ 1880

The Game of Fish Pond, a children's dexterity game, was introduced by McLoughlin Brothers around 1880. *Fish Pond* achieved instant success and was reissued in numerous and increasingly elaborate variations over the succeeding decades.

RIGHT, TOP
Game of
FISH POND
MᴄLᴏᴜɢʜʟɪɴ Bʀᴏᴛʜᴇʀs
Nᴇᴡ Yᴏʀᴋ, N.Y., ᴄɪʀᴄᴀ 1890

RIGHT, BOTTOM
Game of
FISH POND
MᴄLᴏᴜɢʜʟɪɴ Bʀᴏᴛʜᴇʀs
Nᴇᴡ Yᴏʀᴋ, N.Y., ᴄᴏᴘʏʀɪɢʜᴛ 1890

Game of Fish Pond

hlin Bros.
York

GAME OF FISH POND

Game of FOUR and TWENTY BLACK BIRDS

McLOUGHLIN BROS / NEW YORK

Game of
FOUR *and* TWENTY BLACK BIRDS

McLoughlin Brothers
New York, N.Y., copyright 1908

Inspired by the Mother Goose rhyme of the same
name, *Four and Twenty Black Birds* calls on the
dexterity of players to hook a pair of metal wings
on a rod, catch the blackbirds poking out of
the pie, and remove them one by one without
letting them fall. This variation of *Fish Pond*
was produced in smaller numbers and is now a
rare collector's item.

Game of
FROG POND

R. Bliss Manufacturing Co.
Pawtucket, R.I., copyright 1890

Games by R. Bliss Manufacturing Co., a firm
noted for its exceptional lithography, are almost
as sought after as McLoughlin products. *Frog
Pond*, a dexterity game, is another variation on
the popular *Fish Pond*.

❧ 6 ❧

THE
URBAN
EXPERIENCE

The process of urbanization that had begun before the American Revolution accelerated during the nineteenth century. By 1920, according to the U.S. Census, America had officially become a nation of cities and city dwellers. As agrarian life gave way to a new urban culture, the nation's altered self-image found expression in games. With subjects ranging from architectural wonders to street urchins, these games reflect late-nineteenth-century America's fascination with cities as bustling hubs of commerce and culture.

New York City, a booming metropolis and home to many game manufacturers, came to symbolize the nation's prosperity and increasing international prominence. By the time of the consolidation of Greater

New York in 1898, this urban conglomerate of five boroughs with its well over three million residents had become the country's largest, densest, and most populated city. Its skyscrapers, monuments, and feats of technological wonder were frequently reproduced on board games and box covers.

Travel games reflected America's growing tourism industry, which was energized by efforts to promote cities as desirable vacation destinations for middle-class families. *Peter Coddles' Trip to New York* provided Americans across the country with a vicarious tour of the city. Players shared in the wonder experienced by the country bumpkin Coddle as he explored the streets of Gotham. Spin-offs included excursions to other urban tourist destinations, including Boston and Chicago. Poking fun at the naiveté of the rural visitor, these games betray the sense of dislocation felt by Americans experiencing rapid urban growth and suggest their collective aspirations for worldly urban sophistication.

PAGE 132
POST OFFICE GAME
PARKER BROTHERS
SALEM, MASS., COPYRIGHT 1897
The Post Office Game conveys the dense cityscape and urban bustle of lower Manhattan. Players travel along a gameboard reproducing the city's streets from the island's southern tip to 23rd Street.

RIGHT
The Game of
PHOEBE SNOW
MCLOUGHLIN BROTHERS
NEW YORK, N.Y., COPYRIGHT 1909
Miss Phoebe Snow was the fictional character—perennially attired in a spotless white dress and gloves—used to promote the Lackawanna Railroad's use of a clean-burning form of coal called anthracite. In this game, players race across the country by train, boarding in New York City and disembarking in San Francisco.

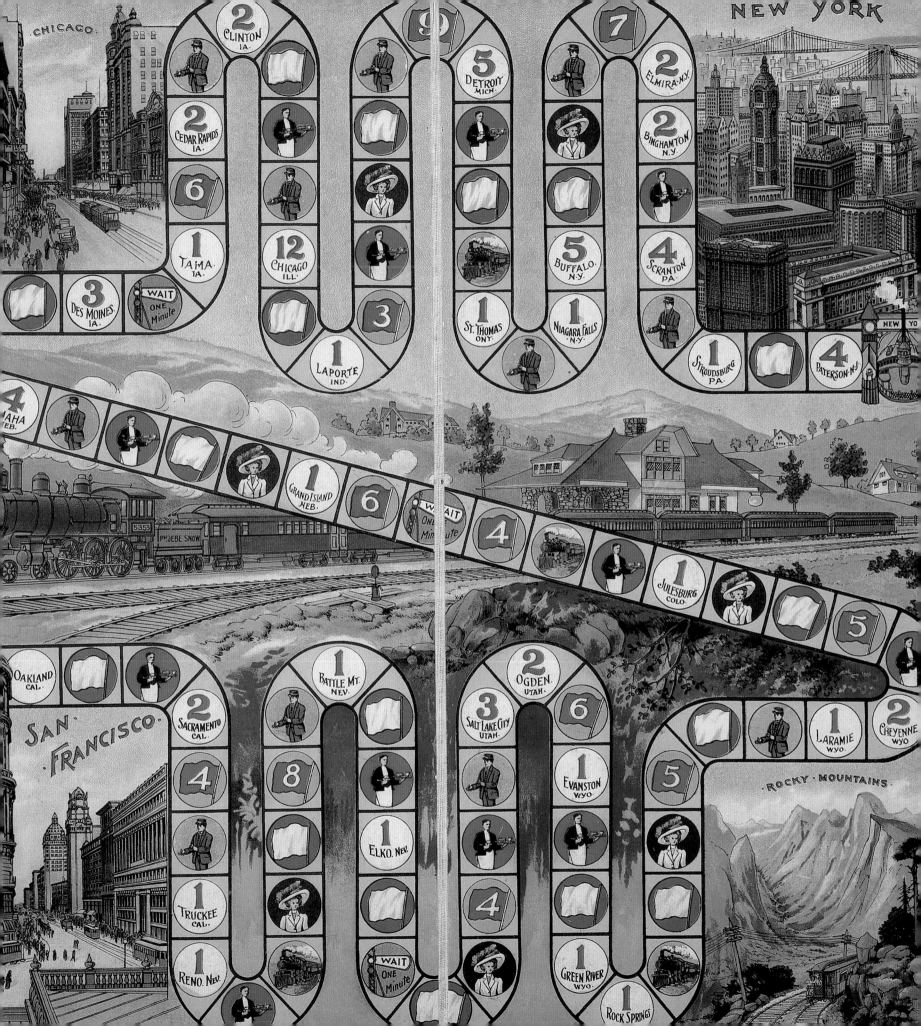

After breakfast, Peter started out to see the sights. A bootblack directed him to the Brooklyn Bridge, remarking he could go over it by paying ——. Peter soon found the bridge and walked out upon it. The sensation was a strange one to him; he could see all over Manhattan Island. On the Tribune building he could see —— above ——; Trinity steeple looked like ——; the Western Union building looked like ——; the shot-tower loomed up, resembling ——. The shipping in the river received a full share of Peter's attention. He told one of the bridge police it made his head feel like ——, and as light as ——, to look down into the river.

TOP LEFT AND NEAR RIGHT

PETER CODDLE'S TRIP TO NEW YORK

MILTON BRADLEY
SPRINGFIELD, MASS., CIRCA 1890

BOTTOM LEFT AND FAR RIGHT

PETER CODDLE'S TRIP TO NEW YORK

MILTON BRADLEY
SPRINGFIELD, MASS., CIRCA 1890

The popular *Peter Coddle's Trip to New York*, produced in many versions by multiple manufacturers, reflects the nation's awareness of the growing urban/rural divide. It also signals a fascination with the sights and achievements of America's largest city. In this humorous word game, players draw cards containing phrases that are inserted into the story of the country bumpkin's urban adventures.

A Singular Mistake	A Glass Eye
A Sea of Turtle Soup	A Stuffed Pig
A Fishing Pole	The Queen of Sheba
A Policeman	A Sloop Load of Clams
A Little Spilt Milk	A Broken Jack-knife
A Runaway Pussy Cat	A Dutch Farmer

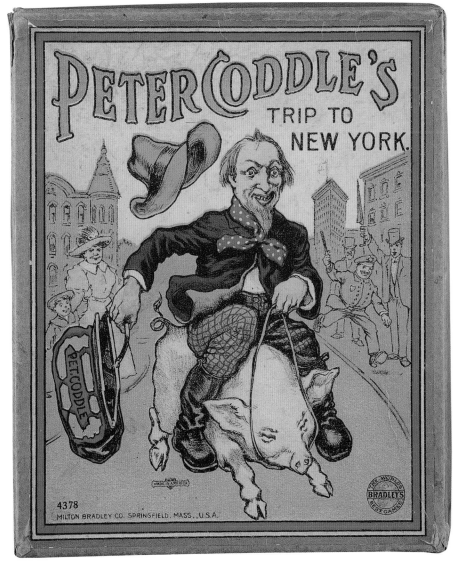

Excursion to
CONEY ISLAND
MILTON BRADLEY
SPRINGFIELD, MASS., CIRCA 1890

The resort of Coney Island, accessed from the rest of Brooklyn by several railroads, attracted a multitude of leisure-seekers to its beaches and amusements in the late-nineteenth century. In this variant of the Peter Coddle game, players read a story about an action-packed visit to Coney Island, filling in the blanks by reading cards drawn at random and, hopefully, having a good laugh.

BOYS' FIGHTING — In Street.
Pay 1 to Pool.

STRONG-MINDED WOMAN.

STREET MUSICIAN.

CHILD LOST. Pay 1 to Pool.

The Game of **CITY LIFE,**
or the **BOYS** *of* **NEW YORK**

McLoughlin Brothers
New York, N.Y., copyright 1889

The Game of City Life reflects America's fascination
with New York as "Sin City." The game's cards
contain vivid illustrations of "the scenes, characters,
and incidents common to life in a large city,"
including the capitalist, the wife beater, the cruel
woman, the street gamin, the rum seller, the
defaulting bank cashier, and the corner loafer.

Jerome Park
STEEPLE CHASE

SMALL CAPS McLoughlin Brothers
New York, N.Y., circa 1885

Located in the Fordham section of the Bronx, the fashionable and luxurious Jerome Park Racetrack staged thoroughbred horse races from 1866 to 1889.

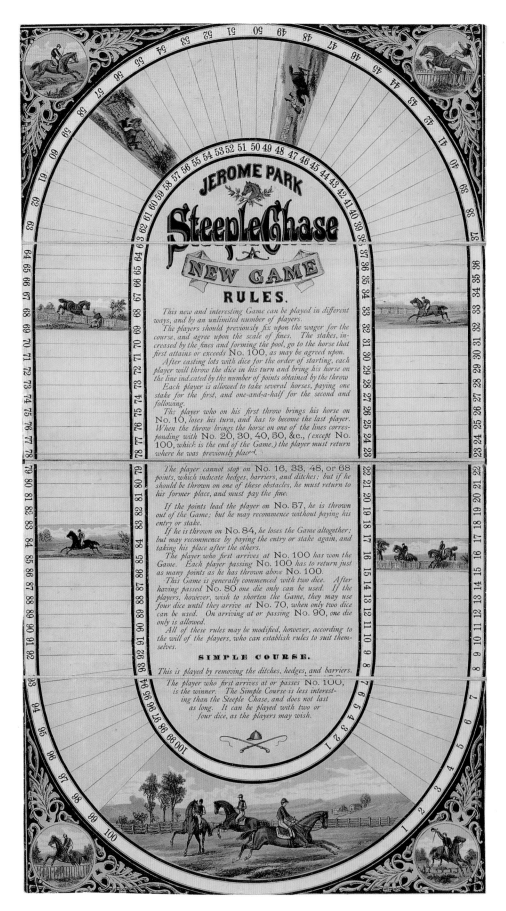

THE YACHT RACE GAME

M<small>C</small>L<small>OUGHLIN</small> B<small>ROTHERS</small>
N<small>EW</small> Y<small>ORK</small>, N.Y., <small>PATENTED</small> 1887

The setting for *The Yacht Race Game* is New York Harbor, where boats sail in the shadows of the Statue of Liberty, the Brooklyn Bridge, and Governor's Island.

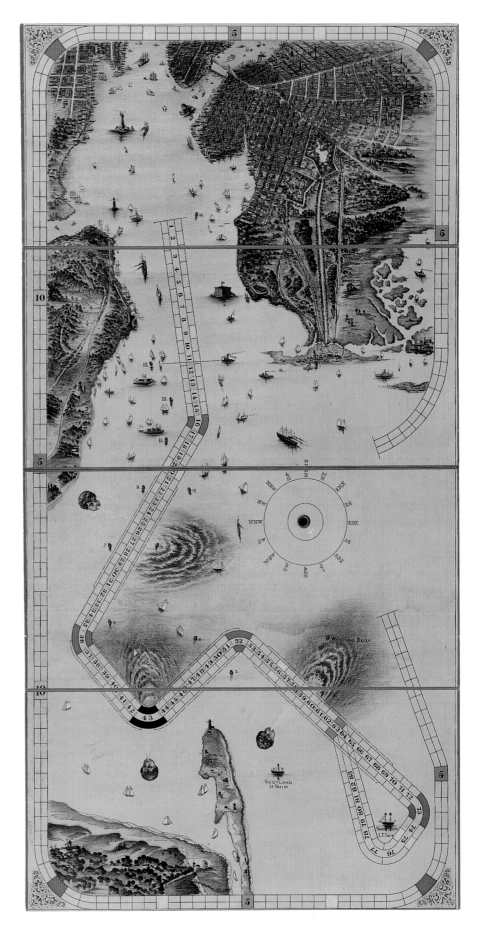

BROOKLYN BRIDGE BLOCK BALL PUZZLE

BROOKLYN BRIDGE
BLOCK BALL PUZZLE

Manufacturer unknown
United States, circa 1883–1900

This challenging combination puzzle depicts
New York's majestic Brooklyn Bridge, opened
to surface traffic in 1883, and the East River,
teeming with steamships and sailing vessels.

RIVAL POLICEMEN
McLoughlin Brothers
New York, N.Y., copyright 1896

With the vivid graphics and oversize box typical of McLoughlin Brothers' best work, *Rival Policemen* is highly coveted by today's board game collectors. Players representing rival police forces compete to capture the greatest number of crooks roaming the city's streets. *Rival Policemen* was inspired by a tense period in New York City's history when a state-controlled police force and the city's police worked simultaneously (but not necessarily cooperatively) to protect the city.

CATS on the WALL
McLoughlin Brothers
New York, N.Y., circa 1900

In turn-of-the-century cities, wild cats proliferated, feeding on the garbage and rats that the authorities consistently failed to remove. Since alley cats were considered pests, few blinked an eye at the way street kids used them for target practice.

The Popular Game of BROADWAY
Parker Brothers
Salem, Mass., copyright 1917

The game of *Broadway* celebrates four of the historic thoroughfare's architectural landmarks: the Metropolitan Life Tower (1909), the Times Tower (1903), the Flatiron Building (1902), and the Woolworth Building (1913). The game offers players the thrill of the big city within the comforts of the parlor—a perfect armchair traveling experience.

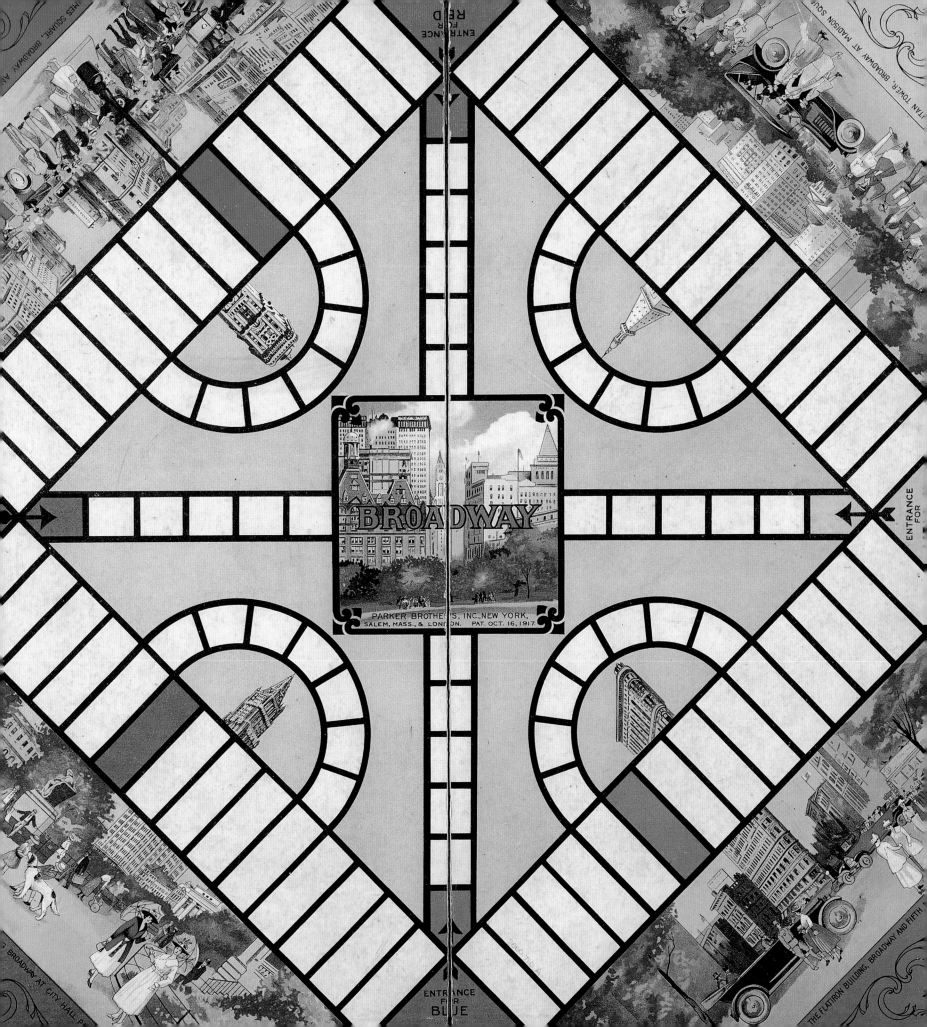

7

'ROUND *THE* WORLD

The optimism and adventurousness of a rapidly expanding nation were vividly expressed in American board games of the late-nineteenth century. Contemporary technological innovations—particularly the Erie Canal (1825), the telegraph (1844), and the transcontinental railroad (1869)—improved communication, stimulated westward expansion, encouraged travel, and helped America forge a national identity. Board games celebrated these achievements, while offering Americans the opportunity to journey across their vast nation without ever leaving the parlor. The railroad—probably the most significant transportation advancement driving territorial expansion and industrial growth—became a favorite subject of board games. The boards of many games based on travel and mail themes graphically depict the newly created web of railroad routes that crisscrossed the country.

By the end of the century, Americans had traveled beyond their national borders in unprecedented numbers. Those unable to make such trips, or eager to relive expeditions taken, experienced the thrill of travel vicariously, through games. Many games of exploration were inspired by contemporary literature, such as Jules Verne's *Around the World in Eighty Days* (1873), or by current events, like Admiral Robert E. Peary's 1909 expedition to the North Pole. Regardless of their specific theme, all American games based on travel and exploration are distinguished by a pervasive spirit of enterprise and adventure.

PAGE 146 (DETAIL) AND RIGHT

Game of
RACE AROUND THE WORLD
MCLOUGHLIN BROTHERS
NEW YORK, N.Y., COPYRIGHT 1898

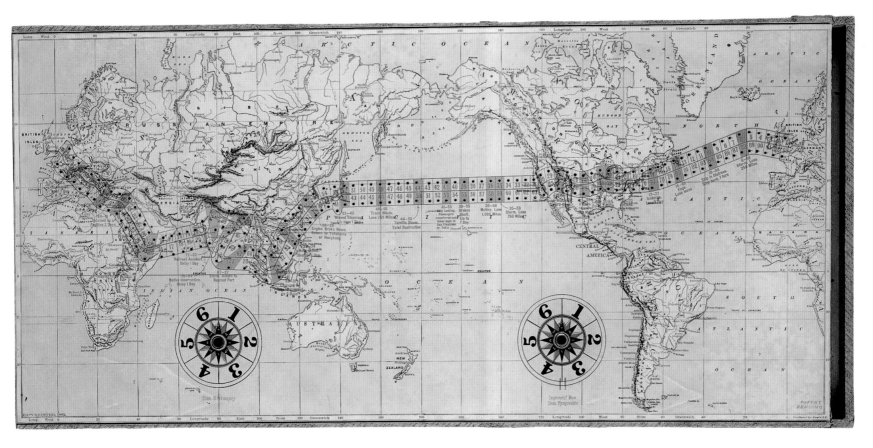

GAME OF TRIP ROUND THE WORLD

Copyright 1897 by McLoughlin Bros. N.Y.

Game of
TRIP 'ROUND THE WORLD
McLoughlin Brothers
New York, N.Y., copyright 1897

Game of
TO THE NORTH POLE BY AIRSHIP
McLoughlin Brothers
New York, N.Y., copyright 1897

Probably inspired by the failed attempt of Swedish explorer Salomon Andrée in 1897 to reach the arctic by balloon, *To the North Pole by Airship* challenges players to successfully navigate the make-believe skies above the icy polar cap.

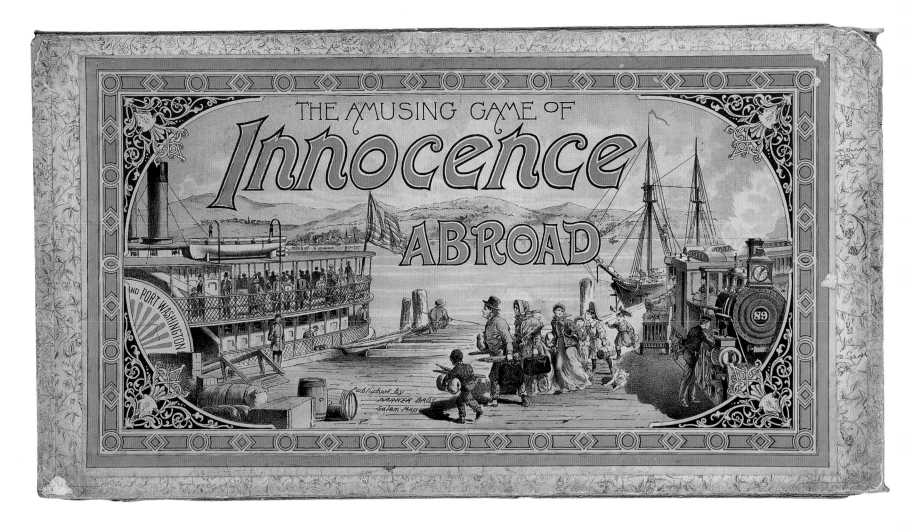

The Amusing Game of
INNOCENCE ABROAD

PARKER BROTHERS
SALEM, MASS., CIRCA 1888

Travelers fortunate enough to visit Paris in the late 1880s witnessed the completion of the Eiffel Tower. Those who stayed at home could experience an overseas journey through Parker Brothers' popular travel game *Innocence Abroad*. The game takes its title from Mark Twain's humorous travelogue *The Innocents Abroad, or the New Pilgrims' Progress* (1869).

THE HORSELESS CARRIAGE RACE

McLoughlin Br...
·NEW YORK·

ABOVE AND TOP RIGHT

ABOVE AND TOP RIGHT
The HORSELESS CARRIAGE RACE
McLoughlin Brothers
New York, N.Y., copyright 1900

Just before the turn of the twentieth century, a noisy new mode of transportation entered the American streetscape. The automobile, also known as the "horseless carriage," allowed restless Americans to travel and experience their nation at "top" speed. In *The Horseless Carriage Race* players using metal car playing pieces "race" across North America following a path that leads them through major hubs like New York City, New Orleans, Mexico City, Los Angeles, and Quebec.

BOTTOM RIGHT
Game of UNCLE SAM'S MAIL
McLoughlin Brothers
New York, N.Y., copyright 1893

Uncle Sam's Mail celebrates America's efficient postal system, which transported mail around the country by horseback, stagecoach, steamboat, and railroad. The goal of *Uncle Sam's Mail*, played on a board depicting a map of the United States crisscrossed by railroad tracks, is to negotiate the routes for the speediest mail delivery.

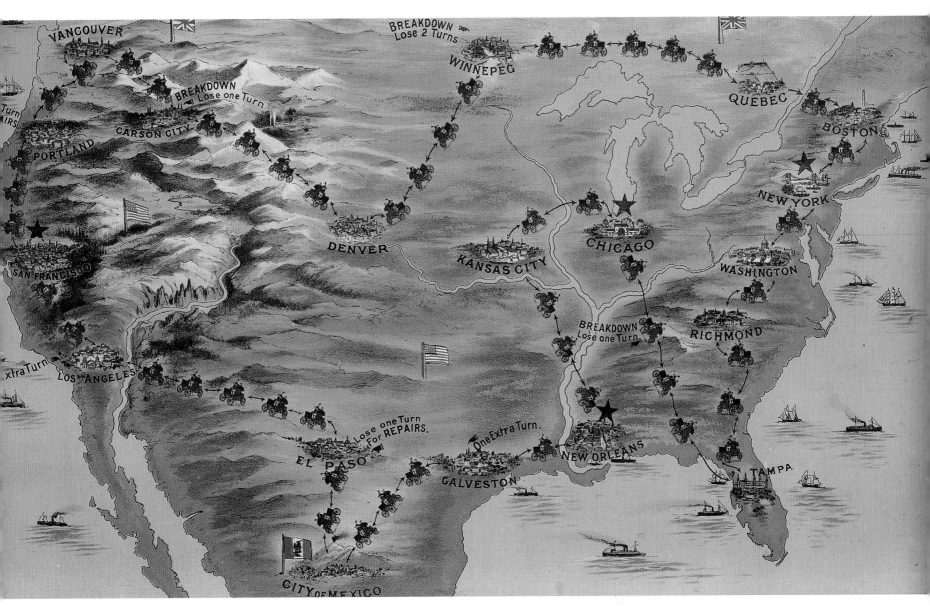

'ROUND THE WORLD
with NELLIE BLY

McLoughlin Brothers
New York, N.Y., copyright 1890

This game is based on the adventures of Elizabeth Cochrane, an American journalist known by her pseudonym Nellie Bly, who traveled around the world in an attempt to break the fictional record established by the character Phineas Fogg in Jules Verne's *Around the World in Eighty Days*. The New York *World* initiated the enterprise and kept its readers informed of Bly's progress with daily articles and pictures. She sailed from New York on November 14, 1889, and completed her journey 'round the world in seventy-two days, six hours, eleven minutes, and fourteen seconds.

SELECTED BIBLIOGRAPHY

BRADEN, DONNA R. *Leisure and Entertainment in America.* Dearborn, Mich.: Henry Ford Museum and Greenfield Village, 1988.

CALVERT, KARIN. *Children in the House: The Material Culture of Early Childhood, 1600-1900.* Boston: Northeastern University Press, 1992.

FREITAG, PETER J. "Playing the American Dream: The Values of Industrial Society as Expressed by Board and Card Games." *Ephemera Journal 6* (1993): 21-39.

JENSEN, JENNIFER. "Teaching Success through Play: American Board and Table Games, 1840-1900." *Antiques* 160 (December 2001): 812-19.

KAYYEM, MARISA, and PAUL STERNBERGER. *Victorian Pleasures: Nineteenth-Century American Board and Table Games from the Liman Collection.* Exh. cat. New York: The New-York Historical Society, 1992.

LOVE, BRIAN, comp. *Great Board Games.* New York: Macmillan Publishing Co., Inc., 1979.

PARLETT, DAVID. *The Oxford History of Board Games.* Oxford: Oxford University Press, 1999.

SHEA, JAMES J. as told to CHARLES MERCER. *It's All in the Game.* New York: G. P. Putman's Sons, 1960.

STEVENSON, LOUISE L. *The Victorian Homefront.* New York: Twayne Publishers, 1991.

WHITEHILL, BRUCE. *Games: American Boxed Games and Their Makers, 1822-1992, with Values.* Radnor, Penn.: Wallace-Homestead Book Company, 1992.

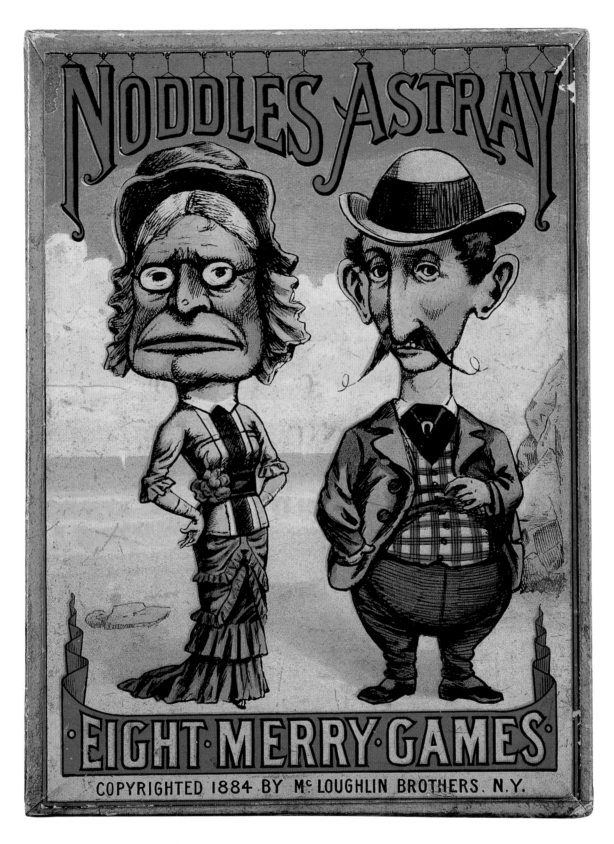

NODDLES ASTRAY:
Eight Merry Games
McLoughlin Brothers
New York, N.Y., copyright 1884